M000033122

Moshe Dayan

MARTIN VAN CREVELD

WEIDENFELD & NICOLSON

Weidenfeld & Nicolson
The Orion Publishing Group Ltd
Orion House, 5 Upper Saint Martin's Lane, London WC2H 9EA

Copyright © Martin van Creveld 2004
First published 2004

All rights reserved. No part of this book may be reproduced or
transmitted in any form or by any means electronic or mechanical
including photocopying recording or any information storage and
retrieval system without permission in writing from the Publisher.

Martin van Creveld has asserted his right to be identified as the
author of this work.

The maps on pp. 89, 134, 137, 166 and 169 in this book are based on
those prepared by Michael Miller for Martin van Creveld's *The Sword
and the Olive: A Critical History of the Israel Defense Force* (New York:
PublicAffairs, 1998, 2002).

Cartography by Peter Harper

British Library Cataloguing-in-Publication Data
A catalogue record for this book is available from the British Library

ISBN 0-297-84669-8

Distributed in the United States by
Sterling Publishing Co. Inc., 387 Park Avenue South, New York,
NY 10016-8810

Printed in Great Britain by Butler & Tanner Ltd, Frome and London

Contents

Maps

Chronology

AD 132–35   The end of the Bar-Kochba Revolt against the Romans marks the beginning of the Diaspora period.

1860s   Earliest Zionist leaders visit the land of Israel.

1880s   The *Biluyim*, a group of Zionist immigrants comparable to *Mayflower* pilgrims, arrive in the land of Israel.

1907   First Jewish self-defence organization, called *Hashomer* (The Guard), established in the land of Israel.

1915   20 May: Moshe Dayan born at Degania.

1917   2 November: Balfour Declaration, promising the Jews a 'national home', issued.

1919–21   Large-scale rioting by local Arab population, especially in Galilee.

1920   Hagana, a countrywide Jewish self-defence organization, founded.

1921   Dayan family moves to Nahalal.

1929   Conflict over access to the Wailing Wall in Jerusalem leads to large-scale rioting. Several Jewish settlements wiped out.

1935   12 July: Dayan marries Ruth Schwarz.

1936–39	Arab Revolt against British rule and continued Jewish immigration.
1937–39	A series of new Jewish settlements built and protected by Hagana. Dayan gets his military apprenticeship under Captain Orde Wingate.
1938	Spring: Arab Revolt ends. British clamp down on the right of Hagana members to carry arms.
1939	October: Dayan arrested by British and sentenced to prison for carrying arms.
1940	February: eldest daughter Yael born.
1941	February: Dayan released from prison.
1941	May: Dayan participates in British invasion of Lebanon, loses an eye.
1944	Spring: ETZEL resumes terrorist activities against British targets. British High Commissioner in Egypt assassinated. On Ben Gurion's orders, Dayan helps hunt down Jewish terrorists.
1947	29 November: UN General Assembly votes in favour of the partition of Palestine and the establishment of a Jewish state. Effective start of Israel's War of Independence.
1948	14 May: Ben Gurion declares the State of Israel and becomes its first Prime Minister.
1948	15 May: War on Israel declared by Egypt, Trans-Jordan, Syria, Lebanon, Iraq. Invasion starts.
1948	17 May: Dayan sent to aid Degania, under attack by Syrian brigade. Forms 'bird theory'.
1948	June–July: First and second UN truce with '10 days' battles' in between. Mass flight of Palestinians. Having fought the Jordanians and the Egyptians, Dayan is appointed Commander of the Jerusalem Front.

1949	January–July: Israel's War of Independence ends in series of armistice agreements with neighbouring Arab states.
1950	October: Dayan appointed Commanding Officer, Southern Front.
1952	June: Dayan appointed Commanding Officer, Northern Front.
1952	December: Dayan appointed chief of the General Staff Division under Chief of Staff Maklef.
1953	June: Unit 101 created under Ariel Sharon.
1953	October: Storming of Jordanian village of Kibiye; 69 Jordanians die.
1953	6 December: Dayan becomes chief of staff with Lavon as Minister of Defence and Sharet as Prime Minister.
1955	February: Ben Gurion returns as Minister of Defence in aftermath of 'Affair'.
1955	November: Sharet resigns, becomes Foreign Minister. Ben Gurion Prime Minister again.
1956	29 October – 5 November: Suez Campaign.
1958	January: Dayan resigns from his post as chief of staff.
1959–64	Dayan serves as a Member of Parliament and Minister of Agriculture, first under Ben Gurion and then under Levi Eshkol.
1963	November: beginning of the 'battle over water' with Syria.
1964	November: PLO founded.
1965	Having resigned as Minister of Agriculture, Dayan joins Ben Gurion's opposition RAFI Party.
1965	Dayan's 'Suez Diary' published.
1966	July–August: Dayan visits Vietnam.

1966	November: Egyptian–Syrian Defence Pact signed.
1967	May–June: Crisis along Israel's borders. Dayan is appointed Minister of Defence. Six Day War fought and won by Israel.
1968	March: Dayan injured during archaeological dig.
1969	March: Start of War of Attrition along Suez Canal.
1970	August: War of Attrition ends.
1971	December: Dayan divorces Ruth.
1973	May: Dayan marries Rachel Karmon.
1973	October: Yom Kippur War.
1974	June: Dayan resigns as Minister of Defence, but stays on as a Member of Parliament.
1977	May: Begin and Likud come to power following elections. Dayan appointed Foreign Minister.
1977	November: Egyptian President Anwar Sadat visits Jerusalem.
1979	March: Israeli–Egyptian Peace Agreement signed.
1979	October: Dayan resigns from his post as Foreign Minister.
1981	16 October: Dayan dies and is buried at Nahalal.

Foreword

Moshe Dayan lived during the 'heroic' period of Israel's history, and was responsible for stunning victories in Israel's two most successful wars. For most of his lifetime Israel was an embattled small country and the Israel Defence Force (IDF) came to be regarded as the most effective fighting force in the world. Paradoxically, its closest rival in fighting power in twentieth-century history was the Wehrmacht in the Second World War. Now, at least in some quarters, the IDF is reviled, and portrayed by much of the world's press as brutal and oppressive.

Dayan was a charismatic commander, who had no need to contrive a persona by wearing a pair of pearl-handled revolvers (Patton), hanging grenades on his equipment (Ridgway), or sporting two badges in his beret (Montgomery). A black patch, covering an eye lost fighting in Syria in 1941, was his instantly recognizable trademark, among politicians, the press, and soldiers. Such was the adulation heaped on him by the media, that for a while eyepatches even became fashion accessories.

From his earliest days as a soldier he led from the front. However high he rose, he was not content to sit in a command bunker remote from the fighting, but went to see for himself, especially when all appeared to be going awry. As with all experienced commanders, he knew that nothing looks so gloomy as the situation on a map in a command post far from the scene of action. It can truly be said of him that, like Napoleon, his presence on a battlefield made the difference of forty thousand men.[*]

No one is better fitted to write an objective and fascinating book about Dayan than Professor Martin van Creveld. An unrivalled authority on the IDF in particular and warfare in general, he is one of the finest and most perceptive military historians writing today. Among his many books, his ground-breaking work on logistics, *Supplying War*, is greatly superior to others on the subject, as is his analysis of command in war. He understands what motivates armies and soldiers, and what constitutes fighting power, making this the central theme of his work on the comparison of the United States and German armies of the Second World War. He was one of the first to predict the present trend towards asymmetric warfare, the increase of terrorism, the re-emergence of warlords, and the decline of warfare fought by nation states. Professor van Creveld does not hesitate to be critical when he feels it is merited, and has made himself unpopular in some circles in his own country as a result of his uncompromising views on the operational methods and ethos of the present-day IDF. His thought-provoking *Men, Women & War*, questioning the place of women in the front line, is typical of his refusal to pander to popular trends. His account of Dayan's life is equally frank, and his portrayal of his subject's character is masterly.

Martin van Creveld has drawn on many sources for his portrait of Moshe Dayan, but perhaps most revealing are the little-known accounts by two of his mistresses. Women were captivated by him and sought him out, for he was a charming and sensitive companion. Well read and deeply immersed in the study of archaeology, Dayan gained enormous pleasure from the discovery of a few ancient flint arrowheads in the desert, even more than from his military achievements. He admired Arab culture, spoke and wrote Arabic, and unlike many of his contemporaries was far

*Quoted by Stanhope, *Notes of Conversations with the Duke of Wellington*, 2 November 1831.

from being contemptuous of Arabs, so he never fell in to the trap of underestimating their military ability. Despite his background he had little time for Jewish orthodoxy, his interest in the Bible being solely as a source of the history of the Jewish people and especially its heroes.

Hardened by a tough upbringing in a communal settlement between the two World Wars, Dayan joined the Hagana, a country-wide self defence organization, established to protect Jewish settlements against Arab raiders. The Arab Revolt in 1936 was directed as much against the Jewish community as against the British rulers of what was then called Palestine (once part of the Ottoman Empire and mandated to Britain by the League of Nations after the First World War). An early influence in Dayan's life was Orde Wingate, a British officer who established the Special Night Squads (SNS) to attack Arab terrorists. Wingate recruited Dayan for his knowledge of the country, and it was from Wingate that he learned about minor tactics, counter-guerrilla work, and how to motivate his men by his example and by caring for them. His transformation from a practitioner of minor tactics to an outstanding strategist and commander at the operational level of war is a measure of Dayan's intellect and ability.

This study of Dayan is important and timely because we are in danger of forgetting how different the IDF was in the first twenty-five years of its existence, from the birth of the state of Israel until the end of the Yom Kippur War of 1973. Whatever one's feelings about the concept of a Jewish state at that time, the IDF attracted the admiration of many for its brilliant performance, against what were often overwhelming odds both in terms of men and *matériel*. Moshe Dayan personified the IDF of that period; a master swordsman wielding a rapier with dazzling speed. In contrast, the present-day IDF is a bludgeon in the hands of men such as Ariel Sharon, himself once a brilliant, if controversial, practitioner of armoured warfare, but, unlike Dayan, apparently unable to adapt to circumstance. As the author comments, today's IDF, with its new ethical code written by a committee of soldiers and academics, and with its ham-fisted tactics in the Occupied Territories, would have horrified Dayan.

This book is a reminder of how speed, shock, and flexibility are battle-winners, as we saw in Iraq in April 2003. But winning the battle is not all; it is winning the war in the long term that ultimately matters. Moshe Dayan certainly understood this. Israeli policy might be very different were he alive today and in a position of influence. For whereas he may have been capable of ruthlessness, his understanding and sympathy for the Arabs and his appreciation of the tactics of the IDF made him a sensitive and intuitive policy-maker.

An indication of this is the key part he played in meetings with President Sadat of Egypt that led to the Camp David Agreement. He made repeated attempts to solve the West Bank question, believing that the occupation of the Territories was untenable. He warned Prime Minister Begin against Sharon's plan for the invasion of Lebanon, which he did not live to see.

Although, as Martin van Creveld concedes, Dayan's image was shaken by the 1973 War, arguably he did more than any single person to bring about victory out of disaster, by his force of personality, courage, and professionalism. His enduring monument is his leadership of Israel's forces at the height of their power and reputation, in two smashing victories in 1956 and 1967.

As an indication of the respect in which Dayan was held by his former enemies, the mourners at his burial included an Egyptian delegation. He was truly a great commander, who stands head and shoulders above his contemporaries of all nationalities.

Introduction

This is the story of one man – Moshe Dayan – who, during much of his life, was so much in the news that his assistants were forced to turn away journalists from around the world who were always waiting to learn about him and interview him. It is also the story of one people – a people who, for many years, idolized him, seeing him as a symbol of their own determination to survive against overwhelming odds. The life of Moshe Dayan coincides almost exactly with the period when Israel, as he himself described it at the beginning of the June 1967 War, was 'a small country, but brave'. First as a young commander, then as a senior one, he inspired the men in his command to live up to his example. He personified those qualities with which the people of Israel identified: of initiative, patriotism, fighting power, and a readiness for self-sacrifice, even death. Shortly after he departed these national qualities began to diminish, in a process of decline from which Israel has yet to emerge.

During the months in which this book was written, the Israel Defence Force (IDF) was engaged in a struggle against Palestinian terrorists, a struggle it was unable to win. During the decades covered in these chapters, the IDF and its predecessors initially fought against just such bands. They then repeatedly defeated coalitions of Arab countries, the forces of which numbered up to a million troops, armed with the best equipment that one of the two superpowers of the time could provide. To those who recall the days when the IDF was considered by many to be the world's best fighting machine, the contrast is astonishing, and it underlies the whole of this book. Focusing on one man, it tells of the way in which a small force, amounting to almost nothing, fought and grew and grew and fought. It did so until it became one of the most powerful forces on earth; ending precisely at the point where, having become so powerful, it no longer knew how to fight.

Dayan, however, was more than a one-eyed Rambo who strode through the world leaving death and destruction in his wake. In him, death-defying courage was combined with a highly developed aesthetic sense – he wrote poetry of no mean quality. The brutality of the battlefield went hand in hand with a keen sense of humour and, when he chose, both tenderness and sensitivity; qualities that in combination caused men to worship him and women to throw themselves at his feet. The older he became, the more he appreciated not only the joys of war but also the pity, the sorrow, and the waste of it all. Having been born and raised when and where he was, he had no choice but to spend much of his life killing his country's enemies (and watching his comrades be killed by them). Yet on a personal level he was without any hatred for them, and indeed they possessed many qualities, such as stoicism and patience, that he admired. During his years as Minister of Defence he often visited Palestinian notables in their homes. Sitting comfortably under some ancient mulberry tree, he would share a watermelon with them and talk to them in their own language. In doing so he was able to command their grudging respect. Having won their respect, he was able first to work with them – as in setting up intelligence networks – and later conduct negotiations with them.

Already in the early 1970s, just three years after the forces he commanded had won one of the most spectacular victories in history, he started looking for ways in which to return the sword to its scabbard. First he explored the possibility of withdrawing from the Suez Canal. The *quid pro quo* was to be an interim agreement with Egypt. Had he succeeded in pulling it off, the October 1973 War might never have been fought, and the lives of thousands, Arabs as well as Israelis, would have been spared. Only a few years later he was among the first to discern the possibility of peace in the Middle East, a cause to which he devoted the latter, and not the least important, years of his life. First, he made a decisive contribution to the Camp David Agreements with Egypt. Next, perceiving that the Prime Minister in whose cabinet he served had no intention of moving towards a similar agreement with the Palestinian people, he resigned his post as Foreign Minister. He had always despised 'the cocktail shmocktail boys', as he called them, and did not want to give up his independence merely to remain in office. Had he not been a sick man, perhaps he would have carried out his threat to take a box, mount it in the centre of the central square of Tel Aviv, and proclaim his views. As it was, he had only a short time left to live. To the end he remained his own man, seeking neither pity nor praise but simply a place to rest.

The plan of this book was dictated by its chronology. Chapter 1 describes our hero's upbringing and youth, from his birth at Degania in 1915 to the outbreak of the Arab Revolt in 1936. Chapter 2 outlines his development as a young commander, up to and including Israel's War of Independence in 1947–49. Chapter 3 deals with the period from 1950 to 1957, culminating in the Suez Campaign, in the launching of which he played a decisive role and during which he acted as chief of staff. Chapter 4 focuses on the period from 1958 to 1967, with special emphasis on his personal life on the one hand and his visit to Vietnam on the other. Though the visit only lasted a few weeks, his conclusions were highly significant; against the background of recent operations in Afghanistan and Iraq, they read as if they were written not three and a half decades ago but yesterday. Chapter 5 deals with the period of Dayan's greatest glory, from 1967 to 1973, whereas the role he played in the October 1973 War is discussed in chapter 6. Chapter 7 outlines the difficult period after 1973, culminating in the conclusion of peace with Egypt. Finally, chapter 8 provides a retrospect on one of the most unusual careers of the twentieth century and, some would say, of all time.

Many of the sources of this book, including a little-known record written by one of his mistresses, have never before been used in an English-language account. Since most are in Hebrew, and assuming they would mean little to the non-Israeli reader, I have decided not to list them or use them in footnotes except in the case of direct quotes. While some of the sources in question have been published in English as well as Hebrew, in the process most have been abridged or modified. This is particularly true of what is perhaps the most important single source, Dayan's autobiography; not only is the English version much shorter than the original, but it omits most of the documents in which the latter abounds. As a rule I have therefore used the Hebrew, although to give the reader an idea of the nature of the sources used, their titles are given in English.

Although I personally never met Dayan, the stories about him abound. Writing this biography I sought to understand both him and, as far as space permitted, the times in which he lived, with neither condemnation nor praise; excessive praise and condemnation being techniques for which he, himself a much better writer than most military men, would have felt nothing but contempt. According to legend, Oliver Cromwell asked for his picture to be painted 'warts and all'. I too wanted to portray Dayan warts and all; and to do so, moreover, in a way of which he, with his unique combination of courage, guile, poesy, patriotism, and disdain for anything phoney, would have approved. Whether or not I have succeeded is for the reader to judge.[1]

CHAPTER 1

Youth on the Farm

The first *kibbutz* in the land of Israel, Degania, was founded in 1911 near the south-western edge of the Sea of Galilee, less than a mile from the spot where, according to tradition, Jesus was baptized. It was built on land that had been purchased by the Jewish Colonization Association from an absentee Persian landowner, Sheik Majid a Din. The Association also provided the settlement with farm animals, equipment and some credit to tide them over until the first crops could be harvested. Originally Degania had fourteen members, twelve male and two female. All were young, and all had recently arrived from Eastern Europe. As individuals, they did not even own the shirts on their backs. Their common languages were Yiddish, the lingua franca of East European Jews, and Russian, although in time they trained themselves to speak Hebrew.

The country was a remote neglected province of the Ottoman Empire. 'A terrible land, without either water or shade', according to the German emperor William II, who visited in 1898. Without paved roads, let alone telecommunications, distances appeared enormous; for example, travelling to Jaffa, about a hundred miles away, took three days; a journey to Jerusalem all of five. Life was marked by isolation, monotony, a lack of privacy and a certain degree of coarseness. Very little attention was paid to aesthetics, partly as a result of poverty, partly because of a socialist ideology that insisted on an almost monastic asceticism. Apparently the resulting problems affected women more than men and a disproportionate number of them committed suicide, a fate that was later to overtake Dayan's own sister.

Capital being scarce, almost the only way for people to make a living was for them to work the land with the few tools available. Agriculture was understood not simply as a trade but as an ideal. According to Zionist ideology, the Jews had once been a proud people of warrior-farmers. Driven into exile after the so-called Bar-Kochba Revolt against the Romans in AD 132–35, they became a persecuted minority and for millennia were prohibited from owning land. As a result they became a town-bound people of petty traders and scholars; to quote Dayan's own father, 'our Jewish bodies were unfit for a life of poverty in the countryside'.[2] An agricultural way of life was seen as the only way to reverse this process, creating a new generation of Jews capable of standing on their own feet. In truth, this ideal was never embraced by more than a small fraction of those who immigrated to the land of Israel, most of whom chose to live in the towns and continue to do so. Nevertheless it maintained its force into the late 1960s. Only then did agriculture become a trade like any other; and the members of the *kibbutzim* in particular ceased to see themselves, and be seen by others, as a social élite.

Dayan's father, Shmuel Dayan, was born in 1890 to an impoverished Hassidic family near Kiev. Receiving little education, he went to work as a tradesman's apprentice at the age of 13 and experienced first hand the pogroms of 1905; in 1908 he and his sister, influenced by the early Zionist Movement, emigrated to Palestine. He spent the next three years drifting from one settlement to another, working first as a labourer and then as a hired guard, before going on to found Degania in 1911. As his famous son was later to describe him, he had 'three left hands'; he was no more fit for agriculture than a horse for dancing and he could never get a furrow straight. He was, however, something of an ideologue, a quality that later stood him in good stead as he entered politics in a variety of ever-shifting parties, all of which had 'labour' or 'labourer' in their title. He ended up as deputy chairman of the Israeli Parliament. At one time he and Moshe served in it together, the son as an aspiring politician and the father as an elderly one whom no one, least of all Moshe, took very seriously. By that time Shmuel had turned into a kindly old man much beloved by his grandchildren; but as we shall see, he had not always been that way. To the end of his days – he died only in 1969 – he continued to celebrate an ideal that was becoming increasingly out of date and in which he himself, because of his activity as a politician, participated only to a limited extent.

His mother, Dvora Zatulovsky, was also born in 1890 in the Ukraine, but here any resemblance to her husband ends. She came from a family of wealthy traders and was highly educated, having studied at the University of St Petersburg at a time when few women did so. Like many contemporary upper-class Russian youths, Jewish ones included, she was influenced by socialist ideals as represented, above all, by the writer Leo Tolstoy. In 1910 she was among the thousands who attended his funeral, weeping and trying to touch his body. Under Tolstoy's influence she planned to devote her life to helping 'the people' out of their backwardness. During the Balkan War of 1911 she served as a volunteer nurse, a typical mission for an educated, emancipated woman of her time. Later she tried her hand as a social worker in Kiev, only to discover that the people she sought to help were thoroughly anti-Semitic and wanted nothing to do with young Jewish intellectuals. Retaining her ideals but recognizing her mistake, in 1913 she left for the land of Israel. She had been given a letter of introduction to someone in Degania, and to Degania she went. At first the *kibbutz* members did not want her, considering her too delicate for agricultural work, but in the autumn of 1914 she married Shmuel and thus became a member nevertheless.

In later years Dvora was often to find herself on her own as her politician husband absented himself from home for months on end, 'serving the movement', as the saying went. Travelling in Europe or the US, he wrote pompous letters about his visits to various Jewish communities. He would tell her how much he hated to live in luxury – at the expense of the Zionist Federation – instead of in the healthy, if harsh and frugal, atmosphere of the land of Israel. In response, she would remind him what it was like to spend a winter on the farm – 'mud, damp, depression, a black mood, not a clean spot in sight'[3] – and do what she could to make him feel guilty. 'Your letter, which I received today, is insufficient. Insufficient to relieve my loneliness, which is great.' Aware of her plight, he repeatedly suggested that she follow him and move – temporarily, of course – either abroad or to Tel Aviv. But, determined to be miserable, as repeatedly she refused. She cited the most varied reasons for her refusal, saying either that she would feel useless in town – in fact, she was offered a job in Tel Aviv – or that the children's education might suffer. She wanted a husband, but only on her own terms; he, aware of this, would describe himself as 'my wife's little *muzhik*' (serf).[4]

From the late 1920s Dvora regularly published newspaper articles, fairly popular at the time, which provided vignettes of life as she experienced it in their then home, the village of Nahalal. A favourite theme was the position of women in the brave new society they were building. As she herself noted in her later days, this turned out to be an illusion; the more established the village, the more women tended to abandon work in the fields in favour of their traditional tasks within the family. Another popular theme was the need to provide the local children with as good an education as circumstances permitted, since, unlike many others, Dvora did not think that it was enough for them to learn how to raise poultry and care for cows. Amidst all this she maintained her love for literature, often asking Shmuel to bring her books. It was a love her son and daughter inherited. Much later, the three of them would compete to see who knew Tolstoy or Dostoevsky better; they were so familiar with their favourite poets that they could locate individual lines unseen and then recite them by heart. She, too, became involved in left-wing party politics, no doubt glad to get a few days' relief from farm life. She died in 1956, shortly before the Suez Campaign that catapulted her son to world fame. In her own way, she was immensely proud of him. Screaming with pain during her last disease, on one occasion she said that, had she been as brave as he, she would have shot herself to end it all.

Moshe – Hebrew for Moses – was born on 20 May 1915. He was named after Moshe Bersky, another early Degania member who, a year earlier, had set out to a neighbouring settlement to fetch medical help for Shmuel Dayan. On the way back Bersky met his death at the hands of some Arab marauders who were trying to take his mule away from him. The incident was typical of the petty conflicts that went on in Palestine at the time. It had little to do with nationalist feeling, given that the clan was the largest unit that most Arabs recognized as their own. Instead it was simply part of the age-old system whereby Bedouin, living in the desert and the mountains, preyed on farmers, Jewish or Arab. So poor were the tribesmen that they could usually be bought off with a pair of boots; but then even a pair of boots might be more than a family of *felaheen* possessed. The Ottoman police, based in the towns which they seldom left except to levy taxes, did nothing. In 1919–20, during the interval between the collapse of Ottoman power and the establishment of British rule, the scale of the incidents increased and part of Degania had to be evacuated for a short time. Shmuel himself purchased a gun and helped guard his home, now pursuing marauders in the surrounding countryside, now being pursued by them.

Relations with the local Arab population were not, however,

characterized only by hostility. Not far from Degania was Um Junny, a typical Arab settlement of the time. Its population of sharecroppers lived in twenty or so one-room hovels built of mud and straw, sharing them with their few chickens, goats and donkeys and cooking on primitive clay stoves. Both sides had something to offer each other. The Arab women taught the Jewish ones how to manage under the difficult local conditions and, in particular, how to look after poultry. The Jews reciprocated by providing medical help when needed. The local landowners, too, were welcoming. Both sides gave hospitality to each other in their homes and gardens. Returning from the hunt for Bersky's assassins, Shmuel himself stopped to rest with an Arab friend and was treated to coffee.

As the First World War broke out and the Ottoman Empire allied itself with the Central Powers, the members of Degania, most of whom carried Russian passports, became enemy nationals. Under threat of being sent into exile in Egypt, several agreed to become Ottoman citizens and a few even enlisted in the Ottoman Army. However, most preferred to pay a ransom – Turkish officers were easily corrupted – and stayed where they were; had they not done so, then everything they had worked for would have been looted and destroyed. But this did not save them from the arrival of war in 1915. Several German air squadrons landed in Palestine, one of which commandeered the two large stone buildings that constituted Degania. The *kibbutz* members, now with two children among their number, were forced to move into the granary. Between the rooms there were no proper walls, only partitions that one could either crawl under or jump over. To make things worse, in the summer of the same year locusts appeared and destroyed the crops, causing a settlement that was already impoverished to become poorer still.

The surroundings of Degania are among the most beautiful on earth. The Sea of Galilee stretches immediately in front, a huge patch of blue,

usually placid, water. To the east are the wild and forbidding Golan
Heights. On a clear day one can see the Mount of Beatitude, where Jesus
delivered the most famous sermon of all time; to the north-east is the
snow-clad peak of Mount Hermon. The climate is harsh; wet in winter
when the rains turn the area into a sea of mud, but hot in summer when
temperatures can easily reach 38 degrees centigrade in the shade. During
the hours before and after the noon 'hell', as Shmuel Dayan described
it, all outdoor work must cease. Each afternoon at around three o'clock
the wind starts blowing from the west, whistling down the hills, causing the water to become choppy and raising clouds of dust. Whether
because of this or because of the chaff in the granary, the toddler's
eyes, like his mother's, became infected. At times 'Musik', the Russian
diminutive Dvora used, was practically blind, constantly crying in pain
and despair.

For weeks on end, mother and child went in search of medical treatment. They covered hundreds of kilometres, some of it by rail but some
by horse-drawn wagon over unpaved roads, through country that was
not always safe; on occasion, practically blind herself, she had to carry
Moshe over the white-hot dunes and all but died of thirst, heat stroke,
and exhaustion. Various remedies were tried but the disease kept returning, and at one point the child also caught a lung infection. Proper
treatment was ultimately only available in the towns of Jaffa and
Jerusalem, both of which were occupied by the British Army in late 1917
and were thus impossible to reach. Hence it was only at the beginning
of 1919, after the war had come to an end, that Dvora and her son could
travel to Jerusalem to have the problem attended to properly. They went
to convalesce in Colonia, a rural settlement west of Jerusalem. Though the
infection was cured, Moshe's eyes remained sensitive for the rest of his life.
The loss of one of them in 1941 exacerbated the problem; from then on
he was always in fear of going blind.

In the winter of 1921–22 the family moved to Nahalal, a new settlement then being built in the north-western part of the valley of Esdraelon. As previously at Degania, the land had been bought for them by the Zionist Movement; they themselves arrived with little but the clothes on their backs. The first twenty-six members – 6-year-old Moshe was the only child – spent the early months living in a few old army tents, their misery compounded by the deep mud. This was too much for Dvora, then pregnant with Moshe's sister, Aviva. Along with little Moshe and some other women from Nahalal, she moved to Nazareth where, attended by an Arab doctor, she spent the next eight months. By the time she had given birth and returned to Nahalal they were able to move into a wooden shanty. It was only in 1936 that this could be replaced by a proper house built of stone. Even then, the available space was so limited that the family normally ate on the balcony. What furniture they possessed was, for the most part, hand-made out of old packing-boxes, something Moshe himself became quite good at, producing a table that rested on a tree-trunk. To the end of his life he retained enough interest in carpentry to appreciate the kind of wood of which furniture was made and the tools with which it had been crafted.

At the time Nahalal was founded the valley of Esdraelon was a green desert, laced with malaria-carrying marshes and thinly settled by the usual miserable Arab farmers as well as the even more miserable Bedouin. Making it fit for modern farming required drainage works, the largest to be carried out in the country up to that time. The record of the meetings held to decide how this was to be done still exists. Both Shmuel and Dvora Dayan took part, and although she was not the only woman present, she was the only one to open her mouth. Something of her character, as well as the spirit of the times, comes through when she insisted that the houses be built in the valley, close to the soon to be drained farming lands, rather than on one of the more salubrious hills. 'Life', she told her worried comrades, 'will teach us how to look after our children's health';[5] national revival was more important than family welfare. Nor did she hesitate to leave her home for a few days when politics called, even if her children were sick. She would tell them to manage, and manage they did. Almost to his last day, Dayan's way of coping with disease was to ignore it for as long as he could.

Unlike Degania, Nahalal was not a *kibbutz* but a *moshav*, a different form of communal settlement. In a *kibbutz*, everything except personal items – sometimes, even these – was the property of the community and the fields were worked by all members in common. Though each couple was assigned a room to live in, everybody took their meals together. Children did not live with their parents but in communal dormitories; in this way they only saw their parents for a few hours each day and on holidays. By contrast, the *moshav*s made no attempt to abolish the traditional family. In addition to having a home of his own, each farmer owned his own animals and farm equipment and was assigned an individual plot of land. He could neither subdivide nor sell the land without the community's permission, although he was permitted to work it just as he pleased. Only the marketing was carried out on a communal basis.

Both *kibbutz* and *moshav* had this in common: that members were expected to work with their own hands rather than with the aid of hired help, which, following the socialist ideology of the time, was considered to be exploitative. To hedge against the ups and downs of the market, *moshavniks* usually grew a variety of crops on the same farm, cultivating fruit, vegetables, cereals and maize, as well as raising mules, horses, cattle and poultry. Besides being highly inefficient, economically speaking, the system also made for backbreaking work for the farmer and his family. Children, too, were expected to lend a hand as soon as they were able to do so, with the result that they became versatile in many different tasks; from milking a cow to planting a tree, and from ploughing a field to the laying and re-laying of water pipes. Decades later Dayan was to say that *moshavniks*, accustomed as they were to perform miracles even with a rusty piece of wire, made the best soldiers of all.

Moshe first began to receive schooling while living with his mother in Nazareth. He was already able to read and write easily, exchanging letters with his father in Nahalal. After they finally settled in their new home the community hired a teacher, one Meshulam Halevy, who taught all the local children by age group. At first there were no desks or chairs. The children simply sat on mats on the ground and Meshulam would ask them what they wanted to discuss that day; after this they continued learning for as long as their span of attention lasted. Later, conditions improved, things became less informal, additional teachers were hired and Meshulam himself had to go. Still, much instruction continued to take place out of doors. The children were taken on hikes that might last for two or even three days. The focus was on nature – the earth, plants, birds, animals – as well as the Bible, the latter forming the justification for the Jewish presence in the Holy Land; some of the heroes whose stories it told had lived and performed their deeds in the same district. Among the most important ones were the prophetess Dvora and the military leader Barak, both of whom had been active around Mount Tabor, within sight of Nahalal.

Another figure that attracted the young Moshe was King Saul, who had met his death at Mount Gilboa, to the south of Degania. At the age of 10, Moshe celebrated the king's deeds in the local children's newspaper:

> Evening came.
> And Saul was leaning on his sword.
> He stood on his country's mountain.
> He stood over his people's corpses.
> From afar the archers could be seen.

From afar the enemy could be seen.
He knew he would fall into their hands.
He knew he would be tortured.
He knew he would be cast into a dungeon.
He knew his end would be hellish.
Mainly, he knew his people would be dishonoured.
As would his country.
That's why he fell on his sword.
And dropped on to the field, dead.
He lay down with the other dead.
But died a hero's death.
The enemy reached the field.
Seeing the dead, they rejoiced.
But a moment later they were saddened.
Because they had failed to get Saul and his son.

Israel was still at this time a backward country where the industrial revolution had not yet taken place. The soil had remained as it was in Biblical times. The hills were the same hills, the vegetation the same vegetation; Arab farmers, if not Jewish ones, were still harnessing their oxen to the very wooden ploughs that had served their ancestors since time immemorial. Although there is no record of his doing so, Moshe is quite likely to have seen the potsherds that were even then being dug out of several 3,000-year-old mounds around Nahalal. He was going where the Biblical heroes had gone, and what they had done he did. To the end of his life, he regarded them almost as his personal friends.

It was during these years that Shmuel started travelling abroad in an effort to convince more Jews to immigrate as well as to raise money for the community. Left on their own, Dvora and the young Moshe bore the full brunt of working a 30-acre farm. They got up at four in the morning to milk the cows, and only ended their labours after the last milking was over at nine at night. Dvora's letters to her husband are full of mules falling sick, chickens' eggs failing to hatch, rains coming too early or not at all, and so on and so on in a litany that had neither beginning nor end. On occasion Moshe too would write, giving broad hints to his father that enough was enough and that he should return as soon as possible. In the midst of all this, at the beginning of 1926, Dvora gave birth to her youngest son, Zohar. The delivery was a difficult one and she never quite recovered. Soon she was referring to herself as an old woman.

From time to time, in spite of the prevailing ideology, they were compelled to take on occasional hired help. An even greater sin against the governing principles was their selling of products to private pedlars rather than by way of the *moshav*. All this gave the family a reputation for dishonesty. As a 'politician' who toured the world instead of working on the farm, Shmuel was automatically suspect; the fact that he refused to surrender his gun to the community did not improve matters. For her part, Dvora was sometimes considered a double-dealer. Meanwhile, so poor that the family ate meat only once a week, at one point Dvora and Moshe were even reduced to sharing the absent Shmuel's boots. Having finished elementary school, more or less, Dayan was fortunate that Nahalal also contained an agricultural school for girls at that time, whose purpose was to prepare them for establishing new settlements on land acquired by the Zionist authorities. As a result, the greatest hero whom modern Israel produced received part of what formal education he had in a girls' school.

To the highly educated Dvora Dayan, as to many other Israelis to the present day, Arabs represented 'the primitive people'.[6] This was not true of her son, who had grown up in close proximity to Arab children and who soon picked up a smattering of Arabic; though no scholar, in the end he was able to read it well enough to enjoy some of its superb poetry.

Indeed, he admired the Arabs for their hardihood and frugality. Paradoxically it was they who were rooted in the country in a way the Zionist ideologues, his father included, could only talk about. As a schoolboy he often made drawings of them; focusing on their long, flowing robes and their lean, creased faces. Letting his imagination roam, when he was 10 he wrote and published a long story in which he and some Arab youths fought together against an enemy whose identity remains somewhat mysterious. The story ends as he lies in a coma, badly wounded. How his life was saved is not entirely clear. Remarkably, when he regained consciousness it was to Allah, the granter of favours, that he gave thanks. At Nahalal, a socialist community shot through and through with atheism, he may have felt closer to the Moslem God than to the Jewish one; certainly he had no interest in Talmud or any other part of Jewish orthodoxy. Much later, when he was already a Member of the Israeli Parliament, it was said in jest that the reason he did not participate in some of the debates about Jewish identity was because he was an Arab himself.

Imagination reflected reality, or perhaps, for Dayan, it was the other way around. Like so many other Jewish settlements, Nahalal had been built on land owned by an absentee Arab landowner and sold to the Zionist Federation from under his tenants' feet. As with so many other Jewish settlements also, this situation led to occasional conflicts over wells, grazing grounds, etc., as well as much petty theft. Poor as the Jews were, thanks to the modern methods of farming that they had introduced they were usually less so than their Arab neighbours. In fact one frequent form of contact between the children of Nahalal and those of the neighbouring Arab village was when the latter came to beg a share in a sandwich smeared with jam. This acquaintance served him well when he later engaged in intelligence work.

The early years were surprisingly quiet, but from 1932 on the situation changed. First a bomb was thrown into one of the houses, killing a mother and her child. Though this incident remained isolated, blows began to be exchanged and brawls took place. In one of them Moshe was hit over the head with a club. It was wielded by a young Arab acquaintance of his, Abdullah Mustafa, nicknamed Wahash (Wolf); he was concussed for weeks and the dent never healed at all. Typically for Dvora the incident inspired her to write an article in which she bewailed Arab perfidy and used flowery language to ask when it would ever end. Typically for her son, however, he took it in his stride and did not see it as cause for lasting resentment. The way he saw it, no Arab ever did anything despicable to him personally. Both sides merely fought for what they thought was right, killing and getting killed in the process. This made him feel a certain sympathy for them, but it also impressed on him the likelihood that the conflict would accompany his people for a long, long time to come.

Other youthful adventures included 'liberating' fruit from the stores of the agricultural school – throughout his life, Dayan tended to take liberties with public property – as well as learning to ride. Armed with whips, Moshe and his fellow youths would charge the hills around Nahalal, driving away Arab intruders and seizing their cattle, which they were later supposed to ransom. It was on these occasions that he first distinguished himself with qualities of fearlessness, ruthlessness and leadership. He also possessed a native cunning that stood him in good stead; then as always, war was made partly by force, partly by guile. In September 1934 he and two friends undertook a journey, on foot, through the Jordan Valley down to the northern shores of the Dead Sea. Even today the country is extremely rugged. At the time it had no permanent settlements whatsoever and no roads; if ever there was a howling wilderness in which Jesus had spent forty days fasting, this was surely it. Crossing it was dangerous in more ways than one; at one point they were stopped by three Arab policemen who thought they might be illegal immigrants, but they managed to talk their way out. Later they lost their way. Had not the local Bedouin proved hospitable, the adventure could have ended badly, for the youths did not have enough water with them.

Having reached the northern edge of the Dead Sea, they parted. Dayan and one of his companions took a bus to visit Beer Sheva and Gaza, both of which were purely Arab towns, and in Gaza they were briefly arrested for the second time on the same charge. The episode was considered sufficiently important to merit a short notice on the first page of the principal Hebrew newspaper of the time, *Davar*. In its version of the story, the youngsters had set a patriotic example by repeatedly refusing to speak anything but Hebrew to the policemen who arrested them. Perhaps the really interesting thing is that, five years after the riots of 1929 and two before the outbreak of the Arab Revolt, two Jewish youths could feel safe in a police station manned almost exclusively by Arab personnel; whether this was courage or foolhardiness is hard to say. As Dayan himself told the story, he had impudently demanded to know the investigating policeman's name and number and even taken them down in a notebook. Then, as later, his willingness to look authority straight in the face was one of his strengths.

Some of these adventures may have been undertaken to impress members of the opposite sex. Though the agricultural school was full of young women, Moshe found them hard to approach. He was shy, a slow developer, and, owing to his family's economic difficulties, badly dressed in shorts made from his father's old trousers. Although he wanted to be a leader, he was far from being the most popular boy around. His fellow youngsters at Nahalal considered him clever, but moody and unreliable; the family's reputation for dishonesty did not help. When he finally met his first girlfriend, instead of kissing her he talked about the need to keep one's desires under control and one's family life pure. She, however, refused his suggestion that they marry; as a result, they drifted apart. In the summer of 1934 he met Ruth Schwarz. Two years younger than him, she was the daughter of a well-to-do lawyer in Jerusalem. Highly intelligent, quite good looking and well-balanced, she was to demonstrate, in time, a capacity for leadership. Her 'official' purpose in coming to Nahalal had been to participate in an agricultural training course. Unofficially she was looking for a good time, which, as she herself admitted later, specifically included boys.

As a child Ruth had spent some years in London and her English was good. Allegedly it was because of this that Moshe, of whom she had already heard rumours, sought her company. A well-known picture dating from this period shows them as a pair of sweethearts reading from a book, a volume that was very probably part of their studies. Many years later she would describe him as 'an idealistic youth, with strong opinions and a firm outlook, a flaming patriot, thirsting for knowledge and a lover of books, full of tenderness and warmth, sensitive and caring ... [and] an incorrigible romantic'.[7] To her sorrow, she was to find that these qualities appealed to other women besides herself.

Ruth went back to Jerusalem, told her parents she was finished with life at home, and returned to Nahalal to study at the agricultural school. In Jewish rural settlements of that time it was very common for youngsters to live together without the formality of a wedding. In fact, doing so was part of the prevailing socialist ideology, which regarded marriage and women's economic dependence as contemptible bourgeois habits. Her parents insisted, however, so they got married in the summer of 1935. To prove that they were not giving way to convention he appeared in khaki trousers, an open white shirt and sandals, while she came barefoot. This affectation did not change the fact that the parents on both sides were fairly well known. As a result the ceremony was well attended both by representatives of the local settlements

– both Jewish *and* Arab – and by leaders of the rapidly growing Jewish community.

As their wedding gift Moshe and Ruth were given tickets to London, a highly exceptional opportunity for young people of that time and place. Travelling by way of France, on arriving at their destination they rented a room and toured the city by bicycle. She, with her cosmopolitan background and artistic interests, enjoyed their stay and soon found work as a teacher of Hebrew. He, coming from a remote village and unable to speak English properly, felt lost in the great city and hated having to wear a jacket and tie. Her parents provided them with fifteen pounds a month in order that the country bumpkin who was now their son-in-law might study and make something of himself. Armed with letters of introduction to the director, Dr Harold Laski, he was able to register at the London School of Economics even though he did not have the necessary qualifications. He did, in fact, listen in to a few classes, but did not find them interesting; indeed he tended to regard theorizing as a waste of time. In the spring of 1936 they returned home, and in February 1939 their first daughter was born. She was called Yael, after the biblical heroine who, 3,000 years earlier and not far from Nahalal, had driven a spike into the temple of the Caananite commander, Sisera.

Moshe was now a young man, married, but without a proper education and without much of a future. Having worked on his father's farm from an early age, he could have continued doing so; in fact the *moshav* was built on the assumption that one son, generally but not necessarily the oldest, would take over the land. The other children were supposed to establish new communal settlements; or, should they decide to go 'private' and live in some town, manage as best as they could. As Moshe's younger brother Zohar grew up and became bigger and stronger than him, he seems originally to have been 'the designated son'. However, his death in the 1948 War put an end to any such possibility. As late as 1956, Shmuel seriously suggested that Moshe give up his position as chief of staff and return home. If he did so he would be able to teach farming to his own son, Ehud, so that the latter could take over the farm in his turn. If not, then it would be necessary to prepare Ehud, then 15 years old, for some profession.

Although Shmuel, in an article he wrote during the mid 1950s, described the *moshav* as 'a new society without exploitation, democratic with no compulsion, based on true friendship',[8] neither at that time nor twenty years earlier was the prospect tempting to Moshe. For the young couple, life with the parents seems to have been intolerable. Dvora was already beginning to suffer from the heavy depression that was to mark her later years and which her daughter inherited. As for Shmuel, he remained the committed ideologue, preaching to his family and insisting that they stick to their 'proletarian' values. So incensed was he at the 'petit bourgeois' luxuries that Ruth received from her parents – a washing machine (oil operated), a sewing machine, a radio, and worst of all, a dog – that he actually shot the poor creature.

In an attempt to get away, Moshe and Ruth joined a group that was trying to establish a new *kibbutz* at Shimron, a hill near Nahalal. The tight communal life did not suit him; as someone once said, he would have lived in a *kibbutz* provided it conformed to his views.[9] He was still rather unpopular, which led to their first marital problems. As his growing involvement with things military caused him to absent himself from home for weeks on end she sought, and found, emotional support in his chief competitor for leadership, one Nahman Betzer, who wanted her to leave Moshe; she, however, felt 'trapped' in the latter's 'iron fist'.[10] Much later she was at some pains to show that this was as far as things went; whatever may have happened, apparently Moshe bore Nahman no grudge. In the event, the land proved all but impossible to work and Shimron was not a success. Later the hill, which commands a magnificent view of the valley, became the place where the members of the *moshav* buried their dead, Dayan himself included.

After two years at Shimron Moshe and Ruth moved back to Nahalal, working Shmuel's land but living in a separate shanty they built for themselves. In a letter to Ruth, Moshe expressed the view he might end up as 'a driver, a watchman, a farmer, a construction worker, or a *kibbutz* member, or a labor union clerk'.[11] The context makes it clear this did not necessarily mean a lack of self-esteem on his part. On the contrary, he went on to tell her that it did not matter so long as they made enough money to spend cosy evenings together; he would read (mainly poetry), she would knit, and little Yael would roll about on the floor. Considering the poverty of the country, his ambitions were normal for somebody from his background, and indeed until the early 1950s to be a driver was, if anything, considered to be above average. By the time he wrote this letter, however, the Second World War had broken out and everything changed.

CHAPTER 2

Military Apprenticeship

From the beginning of renewed Jewish immigration to the land of Israel in the late nineteenth century, relations between the immigrants and the local Arab population had never been entirely peaceful. Noting the unsettled conditions in the country, some of the earliest Zionist leaders who visited in the 1860s already wrote about the need for 'battle-worthy guards' who would prevent the 'tent-dwelling' sons of Ishmael from 'destroying the seed and uprooting the vineyards'.[12] Twenty years later the *Biluyim*, a group of immigrants whose role in the history of Zionism is comparable to that of the *Mayflower* Pilgrims in the English settlement of New England, included a clause about the need to master the use of weapons in their 'constitution'. Words led to deeds, and in 1907 the first Jewish self-defence organization since the fall of Bar-Kochba was established, known as *Hashomer* (The Guard). At its peak it consisted of about forty members who provided what today would be called security services to the early Jewish settlements throughout the country. During the First World War, with some of its leaders driven into exile and the rest forced underground, it practically disintegrated.

The end of the war brought far-reaching changes to the land of Israel. The Ottomans were gone, expelled by a British Army commanded by Sir Edmund Allenby which conquered the country in 1917–18. Palestine became a British Mandate under the auspices of the League of Nations; the rest of the Middle East was divided between Britain – which, apart from Palestine, also received Trans-Jordan and Iraq – and France, which took Syria and what is today Lebanon. In 1917 the Balfour Declaration, named after the then British Foreign Minister, Lord Arthur Balfour, was issued. Taking the form of an official letter on behalf of the British Government from Lord Balfour to Lord Rothschild, it solemnly promised British help in establishing a 'National Home' for the Jews in the land of Israel; later the document was officially adopted by the League of Nations Council.

Though the Balfour Declaration explicitly said that the Jewish 'National Home' would not be established at the expense of the local Arab population, this did little to calm the latter's fears that their country was about to be taken over by the Zionists. Accordingly, the years 1919–20 witnessed large-scale rioting. This was particularly true in Galilee, a mountainous remote area that was as yet almost without paved roads; some of those involved were not native Palestinians but marauders from neighbouring Syria who had crossed the – as yet unmarked – border to rob and kill. The Jewish response was to found Hagana, a countrywide self-defence organization, in May 1920. Organizationally it was affiliated to the Labour Federation or Histadrut, which in the absence of a Jewish government represented the community. In time, Hagana was to become the nucleus out of which the Israel Defence Force grew.

Thanks largely to the efforts of the first British High Commissioner, Sir Herbert Samuel, the rest of the 1920s were almost entirely peaceful. The year 1929, however, witnessed a conflict over Jewish access to the Wailing Wall in Jerusalem which led to widespread rioting. In the old city of Hebron alone some seventy Jews lost their lives. Several Jewish settlements were wiped out, among them Colonia, where Dvora and Moshe had once convalesced. Nahalal, surprisingly, remained untouched.

Spurred on by the rioting, which it had failed either to foresee or to resist, Hagana grew. By the mid 1930s it had a few thousand part-time members who acted as soldiers at weekends and on one evening a week. Organizationally speaking it was a confederation of local branches. The largest was in the town of Tel Aviv where General Headquarters, consisting of only a few dozen full-time activists, was also located.

At the time, rural settlements were seldom entirely quiet. In the Arab villages every adult male possessed some kind of firearm, however antiquated; in the Jewish ones illegal activities such as the acquisition of weapons went on even during the most peaceful periods. Formally or informally, in settlements such as Nahalal all were members of Hagana from the moment they could keep their eyes open and their mouths shut. Needless to say, British Intelligence was well aware of what was going on. Still, they realized that the organization was directed at the Arabs and not at them. As long as Hagana members did not carry arms openly, they rarely interfered.

The Arab Revolt – at that time nobody thought of the Palestinians as a separate people – broke out in April 1936 and quickly spread over most of the country. From the beginning it was directed as much against the Jewish community as against the country's British rulers; during the three years it lasted it took many forms, including a general strike, large-scale rioting in the towns and guerrilla warfare in the countryside. In many ways it resembled the Palestinian *intifadas* that were to wrack the nation from 1987 onwards; all over the country people were blown up by mines, killed by snipers and massacred with knives. The British response was to launch a classical counter-insurgency campaign. They imposed emergency rule, arrested leaders, cut communication links (and intercepted or listened in to those still permitted to function), set up roadblocks, built fences to protect sensitive installations, mounted patrols, laid ambushes, pursued marauders, searched people and buildings for arms, and tortured suspects. To create fields of fire, and also to punish those who had, or were suspected of having, harboured terrorists, they blew up thousands of houses all over the country. In the end the number of Arab dead reached the thousands, the Jewish into the low hundreds, and the British into several dozen.

Responding to the uprising, the British poured in additional troops to strengthen the units already available. By 1939 their number was to reach 20,000, complete with modern weapons such as armoured cars and aircraft; still they could not be everywhere at once. In addition, most consisted of regular infantry. Neither officers nor men understood the country, its people or its languages; nor, with their superior attitude towards 'the natives', were they eager to learn. Under these circumstances Hagana proposed to put some of its own personnel at the army's disposal. Some would act as an auxiliary police force, helping to guard sensitive spots and thus free British manpower for 'active' anti-guerrilla operations. Others would serve as guides to the British units engaged in those operations. In doing so they would not only help put down the revolt but would get training as well as experience at His Majesty's expense.

It was during his stay at Shimron that Dayan, then a strapping if underemployed youngster, became active in Hagana. His first job was to guide the British units patrolling the recently constructed pipeline which, starting in Iraq, ran towards Haifa by way of the valley of Esdraelon, not far from Nahalal. Local bands would study the movements of the British patrols and, in the intervals between these, would punch holes in the pipe and set the leaking oil alight; making for a most satisfactory flame that showed for miles around and gladdened Arab hearts. From the point of view of his British employers Dayan's greatest asset was that he possessed an intimate knowledge of the countryside, having traversed it many times on foot. The experience, which lasted several months, seems to have taught him two main lessons. First, from now on the only kind of intelligence officer he valued was one who knew the terrain better than he did himself.[13] Second, and perhaps more important, he was able to see the limitations of a regular force attempting to confront guerrillas face to face.[14]

In the spring of 1937 Dayan, now an official member of the Jewish Auxiliary Force and the proud recipient of eight pounds sterling a month, was put in charge of six men and a pick-up truck. Previous Jewish efforts at self-defence had been almost entirely stationary as each settlement set up a more or less fortified perimeter and employed men to guard or patrol it. Now, under the influence of Yitzhak Sadeh, a doctrine called 'beyond the fence' was adopted and the first 'roving' patrols established. Part lout – in the communal tent, he would start each day with a loud fart – part highly educated art-lover, Sadeh himself was a veteran of the Russian Civil War in which he had undertaken various hatchet jobs for the St Petersburg police. In 1922 he came to the land of Israel where he worked as a stonemason; at this time he was just beginning to make his mark as one of Hagana's senior commanders, and his path and that of Dayan were to cross time and again. Meanwhile, the 21-year-old squad commander patrolled the dirt roads around Nahalal by day and tried to ambush Arab marauders at night. He and his fellow 'rovers' were the heroes of the day, so much so that a song was written in their honour: 'The pick-up is driving, the pick-up is here'.

In the autumn of 1937 there was a temporary lull in the Arab Revolt. Dayan was sent to a course for sergeants run, in English, by the British Army. There he encountered 'spit and polish' and took an instant dislike to it. He admitted that it might be necessary for the British in running their Empire, but in the kind of petty warfare he had experienced in the area around Nahalal it was of no help whatsoever. This, too, was a lesson that was to mark him for much of his life. The sergeants' course was followed almost immediately by a platoon commanders' course, this one run by Hagana and in Hebrew. For six weeks Dayan practised minor infantry tactics; learning what to wear when going into the field, how to select and exploit a good position, how to advance unnoticed by the enemy, how to cut a perimeter fence, how to fire small arms and throw grenades. He distinguished himself by his physical fitness – his arms were immensely strong – and by his unorthodox, highly aggressive solutions to tactical problems. What he enjoyed most was acting as a 'red' team. Once, playing this role, he mustered a few comrades and together they infiltrated the base, which supposedly was closely guarded. The guards had not been told in advance; had they done their job properly, he and the rest could have ended with a bullet through their heads.

Some time in the summer of 1938 a 34-year-old British captain, Orde Wingate, came to see Dayan. The son of another army officer nicknamed 'The Terror of the Sudan', Wingate had spent years operating in that country. Unlike most of his fellow officers, he could speak Arabic and also a little Hebrew. More than most of his fellow officers, he was pro-Zionist. Something of an eccentric (on returning from operations he would sit stark naked in the dining room, munching an onion), he was well read, his manifold interests including music as well as Jewish mysticism – he believed that the Zionist revival constituted a fulfilment of the Biblical promise. To the Zionist leaders he became known as 'The Friend'. His superior, General Archibald Wavell, who was later to command against Rommel in the Western Desert, was impressed by him and allowed him to set up the SNS (Special Night Squads), a mobile unit, perhaps a hundred strong, charged with rooting out Arab terrorism in the northern part of the country.

The SNS needed local guides, and it was for this reason that Wingate sought out Dayan. During the next few months his men, part Jewish and part British, roamed throughout Esdraelon and lower Galilee, carrying out their task with ruthless efficiency. It was from Wingate that Dayan,

who considered him 'a genius', learnt how a commander might motivate his men by always moving in front and making sure they got a cup
of hot chocolate after their return from a hard night's work; how to cross
unfamiliar terrain at night by using stars and maps; how to select a location for setting an ambush; and how to achieve surprise by ruses such
as putting a car's red tail-lights in front. There were also other lessons,
less savoury but necessary, such as how to kill without compunction;
how to interrogate prisoners by shooting every tenth man to make the
rest talk; and how to deter future terrorists by pushing the heads of
captured ones into pools of oil and then freeing them to tell the story.

In November 1938 several new Jewish settlements were built along the
border between the land of Israel and Lebanon. The westernmost one
was Hanita, then a mass of bare rocks and now a thriving *kibbutz*. A
convoy of trucks carried the prefabricated wooden parts of a fortified
compound to the selected site. Once there these were rapidly erected and
filled with concrete, a system known as 'wall and watchtower' and so
designed as to result in a settlement capable of defending itself within
twenty-four hours. Though the land on which Hanita was built had been
purchased by the Jewish Agency, the surrounding area was purely Arab.
To cover the enterprise Hagana sent a hundred men under Yitzhak Sadeh,
this being the largest Jewish armed force ever assembled until then. One
of Sadeh's deputies was Moshe Dayan. The other was Yigal Allon. Two
years younger than Dayan, like him he had grown up in the valley of
Esdraelon. They had been students together at the Hagana officer course.

The first days at Hanita were spent in the usual skirmishes with local
Arab bands, killing and being killed. In one 'battle', 500 rounds were
fired, a vast amount of ammunition for those days. Wingate himself
came to lend a hand. He condemned static defence and recommended a
more active strategy. Later Dayan was put in charge of a home-made
armoured car that drove along the dangerous road between Hanita and

the nearest Jewish settlement, Nahariya, bringing supplies and evacuating the wounded. The experience was important because, until he was given a motorized battalion in the 1948 War, it constituted the one and only time he commanded 'armour'. Nor was Dayan the only Hagana commander who, by force of circumstances, learnt his business in the hardest way possible: namely, at the cost of his men's blood.

Spring found him back with the SNS, the commander of which was, however, soon moved out of the country on suspicion of being too pro-Zionist. By that time, the Arab Revolt was dying out. This was partly because the Palestinian Arab community was exhausted by three years of more or less continuous small-scale fighting and the vast economic damage it had suffered; and partly because, with the Second World War coming soon, the British wanted peace in their Middle-Eastern backyard. In the event, peace was achieved by the notorious White Book which was published by His Majesty's Government in May 1939. It effectively reneged on the Balfour Declaration – which, it will be remembered, had promised a 'National Home' for the Jews – and accepted most of the Palestinian Arab demands. Just as the Holocaust was about to get under way, Jewish immigration and land-purchase were subject to severe limitations; in addition, the Palestinian Arabs were promised 'evolution towards independence' within ten years.

The leader of the Jewish Community was David Ben Gurion. He headed the largest party (MAPAI, the grandfather of today's Labour Party) and also served as chief of the Jewish Agency. He promised 'to fight the White Book as if there were no War, and fight the War [against Nazi Germany] as if there were no White Book'. In practice, the years 1939–45 found him mostly on the British side, doing what he could to mobilize the Jewish community on behalf of the Imperial war effort. His conciliatory policies were not, however, adopted by all the members of the Jewish community, and specifically, the right-wing ETZEL.

ETZEL (acronym for National Military Organization) had been founded only a few years earlier by a Jerusalem student of classical history, Avraham Stern. During the Arab Revolt it had waged a private war, introducing car bombs into Arab markets, waylaying Arab cars and in general answering terror with terror. Now it directed its efforts against the British, killing individual soldiers, blowing up installations, and raiding bases to obtain arms. Like so many occupiers before and after them, the British responded with intelligence work, checkpoints, curfews, ambushes and raids. They also clamped down on the Jews' right to carry arms, a practice which, as long as the revolt lasted, they had tolerated and even encouraged.

The beginning of October 1939 found Dayan – again, together with Allon – acting as instructor in an officer course run by Hagana at Yavniel, not far from the Sea of Galilee. By this time the Arab Revolt had ended and the British were trying to reinforce their rule by confiscating arms from the civilian population. Two British officers visited the base and discovered their weapons. As a precautionary measure, Hagana Headquarters decided to evacuate the base. Instructors and trainees split into two groups. The smaller one, commanded by Allon, got through. However, the departure of the larger one, which included Dayan and forty-two other men, was delayed; daylight found them still on the move. They ran into a British patrol – the troops were Arabs from the country East of the Jordan – which stopped them and ordered them to surrender. Later there was some debate as to whether Dayan, who with a comrade had been the first to encounter the patrol, could have warned the group's commander, 30-year-old Moshe Carmel, and whether, given the balance of forces on both sides, the surrender was necessary at all. Perhaps a clue may be found in the handwritten note he was able to pass to Ruth, back in Nahalal.[15] His understanding of the situation was that he and his comrades had been arrested on 'a very light charge' of possessing arms.

Expecting little or no punishment from people with whom, a few months earlier, they had been allied, they did not want to risk a shoot-out.

The British did not see things that way. The group was taken to Acre and housed in an old Turkish fortress that served as a prison. Dayan was the second to be interrogated. His predecessor had followed standard orders, refusing to answer questions and demanding access to a lawyer; as his reward, he was beaten up until he fainted, before being thrown back into the cell that held them all. Faced with the same fate and worse – his interrogators, after satisfying themselves that he had a family, threatened they would leave Ruth a widow and Yael an orphan – Dayan decided to play the game differently. Instead of remaining silent, he explained that they were members of Hagana, i.e. not of ETZEL, the group the British were really after at that time. As he had done five years earlier at Gaza, he also threatened that his comrades 'outside' would get anybody who raised a stick at him. The tactic worked. Not everybody thought his disregard of standing orders was honourable or correct, but most agreed that it saved the rest of the group from being tortured.

The trial, which took place at the end of the same month, led to a death sentence for one of the men – who was accused of having aimed a weapon at one of the arresting troops – and ten-year prison terms for the rest. Later these sentences were commuted: the death sentence was replaced by ten years imprisonment and the ten-year prison terms were cut to five; there is some evidence that, had the Jewish Agency agreed that they join a British commando unit, they would all have been released immediately. Dressed in prison garb, they were held in a single large room with just one bucket to serve as a toilet. Dayan was not the most senior man in the group; partly because his English was fair and partly because of his ability to look his jailers straight in the eye, however, he soon found himself representing the rest to the prison authorities. They demanded better food, the right to warm underwear, the right to receive newspapers and to study. Their acquaintances outside seconded their demands, most of which were eventually met. Judging by his letters to Ruth, which were written on toilet paper and smuggled out of the prison, he himself was surprised by his capacity for leadership. 'You cannot imagine how much people here love and respect me', he told her; 'nothing like this has ever happened to me in any company I have been in'.[16]

Acre prison was holding ETZEL men as well as Arab terrorists and ordinary criminals. Unlike some of his fellow Hagana men, who called them 'the scum of the earth',[17] Dayan did not hate or despise these people but tried to understand them and establish a good relationship with them. In one of his letters he described how they and he had celebrated the Moslem feast of *Id el Fitr*; stuffing themselves with all the food they could eat and talking endlessly about politics. He was particularly attracted to a group known as the Kassamites, or bearded ones. These were followers of one Sheik Izz-a-Din Kassam, an Arab schoolteacher turned terrorist who had been killed by the British some years previously; much later, he was to become the patron-saint of the modern Islamic terrorist group, Hamas. Like him, they had left their families to fight the foreigners occupying their country, seeking no reward but the right to live according to their beliefs, but they faced far harsher punishment. Whereas the British considered the Jews 'a semi-civilized race',[18] they treated the Arabs much more roughly. Dayan, who observed them at close quarters, noted how stoically those on death row met their fate; it was the screams and wailing of their families that were hard to bear. Not all the Arabs were sentenced to death, though, and in 1942 Dayan even attended the wedding of the sister of a man who had been released.

In February 1940 he helped smuggle food into the prison, was caught, and spent two days in isolation. To Ruth he wrote that 'I did not inform you of this, because it is hard to explain how much nothing such a cell is; in fact those days were the best I have had, recently, because the wardens outdid themselves in bringing me food and nice things to eat'.[19] A few days later the prisoners were transferred from the fortress to a nearby camp, where conditions were better and they were given agricultural work to do; as the prisoners' representative, Dayan himself only worked as much as he pleased. Though he tried to keep up his spirits, time stretched endlessly. Ruth was finding it very hard to manage. He felt guilty about the food she brought him during her visits, and at one point forbade her to bring more. Apparently she felt unappreciated: 'My girl', he once wrote, 'don't be so sorry and don't be angry at me just because you sometimes imagine I do not pay you sufficient attention'.[20] On 4 February 1941 he wrote that 'sometimes I wonder that you are still writing regularly. For me, here, you two are everything and the more time passes the dearer you are... life outside looks more and more remote, and you are the only anchor. But you have your whole life and is the link with me still strong?'[21] Thirteen days later, without being given any reason and with only twenty-four hours' notice, he and his comrades were released.

The world into which he emerged was very different from the one he had left fifteen months previously. The Second World War was in full swing, and was about to reach the land of Israel. Italian aircraft had already bombarded Tel Aviv as well as the oil-refineries at Haifa; now the Germans were preparing to go on the offensive both in the Balkans and in North Africa. By June they had occupied Crete and invaded Egypt, bringing the war dangerously close. The British High Command began considering a retreat to Syria and from there to Iraq; in preparation for such a move, they agreed to provide Hagana with money and equipment to set up a force of Jewish volunteers. They were known as PALMACH – short for Shock Companies – and charged with waging guerrilla warfare behind Axis lines. Sadeh, who was in charge, appointed Dayan and

Allon as two of his six company commanders. In the event Dayan was only destined to serve in PALMACH for a very short time, a fact that decisively affected his career.

From the British point of view, the task immediately ahead was the occupation of Syria (which included Lebanon, and was ruled by the Vichy French) by way of freeing their rear and/or preparing the way for an eventual retreat to Iraq. Once again they needed guides, and Dayan and his fellow ex-SNS men fitted the mission. He had spent the months since his release working at Nahalal and playing with Yael (who, as he later wrote with a typical touch of humour, 'really was more cute than all the other children').[22] Now he went back to Hanita to organize and train a unit consisting of thirty hand-picked men, among whom was a 19-year-old named Yitzhak Rabin. Dayan would not have been Dayan, though, had he not taken a personal part in the operation. Accompanied by an Arab guide he spent about ten days and nights on Lebanese territory, reconnoitering roads and bridges in preparation for the coming invasion.

Twenty-four hours before the British started their advance, Dayan and his Arab comrade discovered a new road that seemed better suited for the purpose at hand – only to be told by Sadeh that they were now too late since the invading forces were already on the move. Along with five other Hagana members, ten Australian soldiers, and the usual Arab guide, Dayan entered Lebanese territory on the night of 6/7 June 1941. Their mission was to seize two small bridges on the road to Beirut and prevent the French from blowing them up. A stiff cross-country march in the dark brought them to their objective, which proved to be neither guarded nor prepared for demolition. It later transpired that the French had outwitted them, blocking the road further to the south.

At first they were elated at their success, but as daylight approached they became concerned. Located deep in a wadi, their position was vulnerable; should the French counter-attack, they would be massacred. The Arab guide, Rashid, suggested that they occupy a nearby police station which was more suitable for defence. His advice was taken and they stormed the station. Covered by the rest, Dayan went ahead, throwing in two hand grenades and silencing the machine gun that defended the building. They entered the station and went up to the roof, where Dayan set up a captured machine gun. Here they came under French fire, and as Dayan tried to locate its source, a sniper bullet hit the field glasses, causing them to disintegrate. Splinters of these were driven into his left eye, the bridge of his nose, and his hand. With astonishing stoicism, he neither cried nor screamed but simply lay and waited quietly until he could be evacuated six hours later. Even so it was hours and hours more before, following an agonizing journey over atrocious Lebanese roads, he finally reached hospital in Haifa.

The wound to the eye was very serious and took months to heal. Even then, the bones remained shattered. Several attempts to install a glass eye failed and he was forced to wear an eyepatch, which he hated, taking it off as soon as he got home. Much later, as his fame grew, admirers from all over the world started sending him others. In the end he owned a large collection of them; one at least being covered with gold, with a Star of David etched on it. Although he did manage to drive and even walk cross-country at night, he suffered from insomnia and frequent headaches, which made it hard for him to read, and helped explain his preference for the field over the office. As time passed he became increasingly moody and introverted. He kept his distance from the men, who admired him without loving him. Those who thought he loved them were apt to be sorely disappointed; in this respect he differed sharply from his long-time competitor, Yigal Allon. Yet, thanks largely to a sense of self-irony and the crooked smile that went with it, he could be extremely charming. Once a worried subordinate came to him saying he had not been taught to do a certain job. 'Do you think I know how to do mine?'[23] was the answer he got.

In 1941–42, a young man of his background who wanted to 'do his bit' could either join the British Army or serve with the Jewish community's own nascent striking force, PALMACH. There is no evidence that Dayan ever considered the former, although given that both his sister Aviva and his brother Zohar did serve with the British, perhaps this was because he was classified as an invalid. As for PALMACH, it was an extremely close-knit group with definite political views; later it became closely associated with a party to the left of Ben Gurion's own MAPAI, MAPAM. Its leaders, including above all Yigal Allon, who was now second in command after Sadeh, may not have wanted the lonely wolf with the eyepatch any more than he wanted them. With his experience, he was too junior to command them and too senior to be commanded by them.

Falling between two stools, he spent the next year working directly for Sadeh in a joint Anglo-Jewish venture known as the Palestine Scheme. He was charged with organizing an intelligence network that would pass on information from behind German lines should the British withdraw; later he also helped train Arabic-speaking commandos for Hagana and German-speaking ones for British-led operations in the Mediterranean and Europe. In the summer of 1942, more from boredom than for any other reason, he joined a small Hagana group which accompanied a British convoy to Iraq. Dressed as an Arab donkey-driver, he was able to enter Baghdad and deliver some arms to the Hagana cell there. The episode contributed to his reputation as a daredevil and a rogue, which was not, as we shall see, something that necessarily acted in his favour.

Ruth having delivered their second child, Ehud, in January 1942, Dayan stayed at home at Nahalal from the autumn of 1942 to that of 1944. In November 1945 their third and last child, a son, Asaf, was born; much later, Yael was to present this period as the happiest in her parents' lives. Moshe's father-in-law, who early in the war had suffered from financial difficulties, was now doing well by trading in land, and he helped him purchase his own farm in the *moshav*. Dayan's autobiography, which for all its apparent frankness conceals as much as it reveals, touches on this period with a single page. Running as a representative of 'The Younger Generation', he tried to get elected to the leadership of Ben Gurion's MAPAI Party, but failed. At the end of 1946 he travelled to Basel, together with his father who was a delegate, to attend the 22nd Zionist Congress and, immediately after, a meeting of MAPAI. At the latter he gave a speech; however, the fire-eating youngster whose solution to every problem was to 'bomb bridges ... buildings ... camps' only made his colleagues' hair stand on end. He in turn found the sessions had 'neither contents nor grandeur'. Tongue in cheek, he claimed that some of the people he met had almost turned him into an anti-Semite.[24]

Meanwhile, other sources tell us that the tough, secretive, independently minded ex-commando did more than was immediately apparent. It will be remembered that, as the Second World War broke out, Ben Gurion had decided that the Jewish community would co-operate with the British against Nazi Germany. Not all the community's members accepted the decision, though, and by the spring of 1944 ETZEL resumed terrorist activities against British targets, culminating, in November of the same year, in the assassination of the British High Commissioner in Egypt by members of a splinter group called LEHI or Freedom Fighters. Ben Gurion found himself in a position much like that of Chairman Yasser Arafat in relation to the government of Israel fifty-seven years later; either hunt the terrorists down, the British told him, or else we shall do so ourselves using far more drastic means. The unsavoury work was entrusted to Sadeh, now Hagana deputy chief of staff, and to Allon, who had taken his place at the head of PALMACH. In principle, both

Allon and Sadeh supported the 'Season', as the operation was called. However, both drew the line when it came to turning in ETZEL and LEHI members to the British authorities. Dayan's reaction was exactly the opposite. He made no secret of his dislike for the job, but he also carried out Ben Gurion's orders. Many years later, he was to lecture his fellow officers on the duty of a soldier to obey under all circumstances.

The most consummate Machiavellian is he who does not appear to be one. Like both Wavell, in whose army he once served, and Eisenhower, Dayan knew how to appear simple while concealing a complex character and, as often as not, even more complex military–political manoeuvres. Superficially he was the most straightforward of soldiers who said and wrote as he did because it was 'the truth'.[25] To the end of his life, as he outlined in a poem written for his children, he claimed that he only knew how to do two things: to work the land and, 'as the thundering guns threaten our home, return war for war'.[26] In so far as he was no ideologue and despised party politics, the appearance was true. It was also true, however, that no soldier was more attuned to political developments or better understood whom to serve and whom to avoid. He was a master at knowing when to claim responsibility and when to dodge it; as a weaver of intrigues and spreader of rumours he had few peers. More impressive still, his sense of humour enabled him to do all this without making too many enemies. Once the wife of an ETZEL man he was holding complained that having to approach a fellow-Jew was worse than speaking to the British police; he retorted that, if she really preferred the British, calling them would be easy enough. Perhaps he used similar methods to charm Menahem Begin, the ETZEL leader whom he had met for the first time a few months earlier. Perhaps, too, his persecution of the two organizations was not as serious as it first seemed. In any case neither Begin nor other members of ETZEL and LEHI bore him a lasting grudge.

As Hagana prepared to fight Israel's War of Independence from 1946 to 1948 Dayan served as its officer for 'Arab Affairs'; the code for setting up intelligence networks. His first collaborators came from the area around Nahalal, but later his network also expanded over the rest of the country. Very little is known about this period in his life. In late 1947 he was involved in training commandos charged with infiltrating Syria to gather intelligence and, perhaps, make contact with possible collaborators. In early 1948 he participated in several Hagana meetings held to decide the fate of this or that Arab-inhabited area. In April that year a Druze battalion came from Syria to help the Palestinian Arabs, and Dayan was instrumental in bribing its officers so that the battalion would fight on the side of Hagana instead; perhaps this was the fruit of his previous work. Later in the same month he played a part in bringing about the surrender of Acre, the first Arab city that was occupied by Hagana without its population leaving en masse. In the midst of these events his 22-year-old brother, Zohar, was killed not far from Nahalal. He was big, blond and handsome, and his body had been left lying in the sun for several days before it could be recovered. Moshe was summoned and identified him by a scar on his wrist. It was one of the few times when the fiercely independent, unapproachable Dayan had to ask for emotional support.

Probably the mass flight of the Palestinian Arabs, which began around this time, either caused Dayan's intelligence networks to collapse or sharply reduced the role they could play. In any case he was left without a job. At that time his old rival Allon was commanding the entire Northern Front. The *de facto* chief of staff was Yigael Yadin, who was just 31 years old; even Rabin, seven years younger than Dayan, was in charge of a PALMACH brigade operating in the area near Jerusalem. Fortunately for Dayan, an opportunity soon presented itself.

On 14 May 1948 Ben Gurion declared the State of Israel, and on the next day the regular armies of Egypt, Trans-Jordan, Iraq, Lebanon and

Syria started their invasion. It was impossible for Hagana forces, which had just begun to emerge out of the underground and as yet were neither trained nor equipped, to be everywhere at once; the result was a truly desperate situation as the commanders of the various fronts screamed for help. On 17 May, for want of a better alternative, the then Major Dayan was dispatched to the aid of Degania, which at the time was under attack by a Syrian brigade that had driven down the Golan Heights. Degania itself was unimportant except, perhaps, as a symbol. However, only 6 or 7 kilometres to the north lies the town of Tiberias through which ran the only road from the valley of Esdraelon to the Upper Jordan valley. In order to prevent that area and the Jewish settlements it contained being cut off, therefore, the Syrian advance had to be halted.

Dayan brought with him a company of 16–17-year-old volunteers, three light anti-tank weapons and, most important, four First World War vintage 65-mm mountain guns dubbed 'Napoleonchiks'. The latter had only just arrived; being desperately needed elsewhere, they were lent to him for twenty-four hours. Apparently his main contribution was to order the occupation of a small hill on the flank of the expected Syrian advance, thereby putting an additional obstacle in its path. The battle climaxed shortly after noon on the 20th. Two Syrian tanks penetrated Degania and had to be fought off with Molotov cocktails; having waited until this moment, the three serviceable 'Napoleonchicks' opened fire. Taken by surprise, the Syrian troops turned tail, abandoning not just the attack on Degania but the nearby settlement of Tzemach which had fallen to them. Dayan visited Tzemach that night and was impressed by the ease of it all. The episode convinced him that Arab troops could be scattered by banging a few tins, as if they were birds.[27] Dubbed 'the birds theory', this view may have been justified at the time. Much later, it returned to haunt him.

Within a few weeks he was given an opportunity to put his theories into practice. He spent the last week of May and the first three of June raising troops and equipment for a new motorized battalion, the 89th, which was then being organized at Tel Hashomer, east of Tel Aviv. It was a chaotic time: the IDF were just beginning to emerge from the underground and mobilize even while the first heavy weapons, which had been waiting for the end of the British Mandate, were beginning to arrive from abroad. Dayan, however, thrived on chaos. Some of the men he recruited were ex-prisoners; others were persuaded to leave their old units, still others were ex-ETZEL and LEHI members. At that time the latter were being incorporated into the IDF; apparently they preferred to serve with Dayan rather than with their ideological opponents from PALMACH or with officers, such as Major Haim Laskov, who had served in the British Army. Equipment, too, was acquired partly by theft from other units or from civilians. One of those who had his jeep 'borrowed' was the famous author, Arthur Koestler, who was then in Palestine gathering material for a new book.

On 20 June the battalion was sent into action for the first time, but not against the Arabs. ETZEL had brought an arms-carrying ship from France and was trying to unload it on a beach north of Tel Aviv; Ben Gurion, who feared a right-wing *coup* was in the making, sent Dayan to deal with the situation. Riding their half-tracks, he and his men arrived on the scene. They set up mortars and shelled the beach, taking some casualties but forcing the ship to lift anchor and sail for Tel Aviv where a PALMACH unit destroyed it with artillery fire. In the midst of this operation he was called personally to see the Prime Minister at the latter's home. Ben Gurion's American adviser, Colonel David Marcus, had just been killed by friendly fire; he wanted Dayan to travel to the USA to represent Israel at the funeral which was to take place at West Point.

Passing through New York on his return he met Major Abraham Baum, a retired American armoured corps officer. In March 1945, acting under General George S. Patton's orders, Baum had taken a 300-strong task force on a mission to Hammelburg, then 60 miles behind the lines, to occupy a prisoner of war camp where Patton's son-in-law was being held. The task force reached Hammelburg and released some of the prisoners; on its way back, however, the force was annihilated and Baum himself was captured. (Later Patton, coming under critical fire but wishing to show himself unrepentant, presented Baum with a medal.) Dayan had hoped to learn from this 'real expert', well aware that he did not have the experience to command mechanized forces. According to his biographer,[28] Baum emphasized the following principles:

1   There is always a road; use it;

2   Concentrate all your forces even against a small objective; do whatever you can to create the illusion that your force is much larger than it is;

3   Attack on a narrow front, preferably in single column;

4   Use your firepower as much to frighten as to kill – a terrified enemy is almost as good as a dead one;

5   When commanding a small force, movement is all-important – stop, and you lose your greatest advantage;

6   Forget about reserves; use them only to mislead the enemy into thinking you have more forces than you actually do;

7   Use infantry to hold occupied terrain;

8   Keep your armour for the counter-attack.

In his autobiography Dayan makes light of this episode, merely saying that Baum told him that surprise was all-important, even at the expense of preliminary reconnaissance. Once an attack had started, it should never be allowed to stop or lose momentum until the objective was reached. As to the commander, his place was at or near the head of his unit; only thus could he see things with his own eyes and give his orders accordingly.

Returning home on 9 July Dayan rejoined his battalion – years later, the men still spoke of how his appearance, straight from the airport, lifted their spirits. He found them preparing for their part in operation 'Danny', which had been ordered by the General Staff. The objective was to fight off the forward units of the Arab Legion which had come from across the Jordan and stood within 15 miles of Tel Aviv. In its second phase, it would aim east at the central positions of the legion at Latrun or Ramallah. Alternatively, it would turn west with the more modest objective of clearing the large Arab-inhabited area around Lydda and Ramle; twin towns on the way to Jerusalem which Ben Gurion had just described as 'thorns' that he wanted 'cleansed'.[29] The operation's commander was Allon, with Rabin as his chief of staff. Dayan's direct superior was Sadeh, who had recently been demoted by Ben Gurion and whose newly formed 8th Armoured Brigade was to act as the northern prong of the operation. In practice, except for one critical decision, when he co-ordinated with Allon, Dayan was on his own; from his limited perspective at the head of his troops, he did what he saw fit.

His deputy, Yohanan Peltz, was an ex-British Army officer whose formal military training was far better than Dayan's. In his commander's absence he had drawn up an elaborate plan that included artillery preparation – in fact, all they had were some 3-inch mortars – and converging movements from several directions. Dayan, recalling his talk with Baum and reminding his men that they were fighting Arabs and not Germans, decided to dispense with it. He ordered his force of light armoured cars, half-tracks and jeeps to advance in a single column. Only if they met resistance were they to deploy, making use of their machine guns before resuming the advance.

The attack started on the morning of 10 July, proceeding roughly from north to south. Three enemy-held villages were reached and occupied at a cost of only five wounded. At one of them Dayan had to conduct a personal reconnaissance; he zigzagged uphill in his jeep while bullets struck all around. As he was later to note,[30] it was not so much a question of courage as of indifference. Coming under fire, somehow his body refused to shrink as other people's did; on the next day, asked what would happen if the road they were going to take was mined, he answered that they'd all be blown to hell. The combination of extreme daredevilry and a certain dark callousness worked wonders, both inspiring confidence and making the men feel ashamed for not being as brave as their commander. In any case they followed him unquestioningly.

That same evening, still covered with dust and grime, he was summoned to Tel Aviv to see Ben Gurion, who wanted him to take over as commander of the Jerusalem Brigade. He refused point-blank to change in mid battle and returned to his men, only to find them scattered all over the villages they had occupied. It took an effort, some of it none too delicate, to concentrate them and make them ready for action again. Peltz, whom he had found fast asleep and whom he blamed for the situation, he left behind on his own in the middle of a newly captured Arab village. Much later the deputy commander avenged himself by writing his own account of the battle, presenting the national hero as a military ignoramus and a scoundrel to boot. In a way, both charges were true; Dayan was certainly not the first man who, writing his memoirs, claimed for himself feats that he had seen being performed by others. Yet in the end it was he and not Peltz who had the political savvy to rise to the top and, as important, the charisma to carry his men with him.

The next day the battalion resumed its advance, reaching and taking a stronghold by the name of El Tariff. There they found an abandoned armoured car that had belonged to the Arab Legion. It sported a 2-inch gun, a much heavier weapon than any mounted on their own vehicles and one ideally suited for blowing away any enemy positions they encountered. According to his own account, Dayan personally helped tow it away and restore it to action. Later his men accidentally discovered some ammunition for it; as Napoleon used to say, not the least important quality a commander needs is sheer luck.

According to the original plan, he should have attacked yet another legion-held position at Beth Naballah on the way to Latrun and, behind it, Ramallah north of Jerusalem; had the latter been reached, then the West Bank would have been cut in half. However, the topography was difficult. A tank battalion, which should have supported Dayan by its fire, failed to show up, an incident which may have ignited his distrust of armoured forces that lasted until after the 1956 War. Meanwhile, only 5 kilometres to the west he could see Lydda, a tempting target whose defenders did not expect to be attacked from the rear. In his autobiography Dayan presents the decision to change direction as if he made it entirely on his own and on the spur of the moment; in fact he contacted Allon and received his permission. By implication, the attack on Latrun was abandoned – perhaps Dayan, who knew that three previous attempts to take the fortress had failed, did not want to try his luck. As a result Latrun, and with it the entire West Bank, remained in Jordanian–Arab hands for another nineteen years.

On 11 July the attack started, the most notable operation carried out by Dayan during the 1948 War. One company was left behind to guard El Tariff. The other two, with a little over two hundred combatants between them, set out to raid Lydda and, behind it, Ramle, with their 40,000 inhabitants; the defences were manned by local irregulars plus two legion companies that had come to reinforce them. Once again they drove in

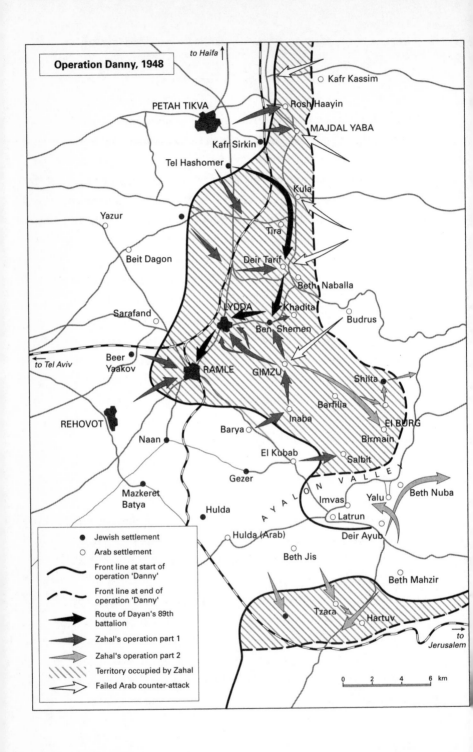

Operation Danny, 1948

to Haifa

Kafr Kassim

PETAH TIKVA

Rosh Haayin

MAJDAL YABA

Kafr Sirkin

Tel Hashomer

Kula

Yazur

Tira

Beit Dagon

Deir Tarif

Beth Naballa

Sarafand

LYDDA

Khadita

Budrus

Ben Shemen

Beer Yaakov

to Tel Aviv

RAMLE

GIMZU

Shilta

EL BURG

REHOVOT

Barfilia

Inaba

Birmain

Naan

Barya

El Kubab

Salbit

Gezer

Mazkeret Batya

Hulda

AYALON VALLEY

Imvas

Yalu

Beth Nuba

Latrun

Deir Ayub

Hulda (Arab)

Beth Jis

Beth Mahzir

to Jerusalem

Tzara

Hartuv

● Jewish settlement

○ Arab settlement

Front line at start of operation 'Danny'

Front line at end of operation 'Danny'

Route of Dayan's 89th battalion

Zahal's operation part 1

Zahal's operation part 2

Territory occupied by Zahal

Failed Arab counter-attack

0 2 4 6 km

single file, this time led by the captured armoured car which they had dubbed 'The Terrible Tiger'. They outflanked some Arab positions and shot their way through the rest. Firing wildly in all directions they entered Lydda where, contrary to Dayan's instructions, 'The Terrible Tiger' became separated and went on fighting a solo battle. Led by a half-track whose driver did not know Hebrew and did not respond to Dayan's orders to halt, the rest of the battalion reached Ramle. Next they turned around – by now many vehicles had been hit and had to be pushed or pulled by others – and forced their way back through Lydda where they picked up the Tiger as well. They lost nine dead and seventeen wounded; the latter included Peltz and two company commanders. The entire attack, the largest that Dayan ever commanded in person, lasted forty minutes. Since they merely entered and withdrew, they did not participate in the great ethnic cleansing that started the next day after another unit, Yiftah Brigade, had come up from the opposite direction and captured the two towns.

Dayan himself took credit for delivering the decisive, unnerving blow that opened the route to Yiftah Brigade and thus led to the fall of Lydda and Ramle. Laskov, who was chief of training and who would eventually succeed Dayan as chief of staff, considered the operation exemplary in its daring as well as its use of surprise, movement, and firepower; since he was unquestionably honest, his testimony carries some weight. Yadin, from his post as chief of staff, criticized its 'wild' character but added that nothing succeeds like success. Others were less sure. Allon, while he did recognize Dayan's share in bringing about the fall of the twin cities, gave most of the credit to Yiftah Brigade. Writing his memoirs thirty years later, Rabin was less charitable still. Dayan, he says,[31] had carried out a raid but failed to hold Lydda, let alone Ramle further down the road. Instead, having suffered considerable loss, he was forced to withdraw; on the next day Arab armoured cars were still patrolling Lydda.

The decisive voice was that of Ben Gurion. His own military experience was limited to a few months' service in a mule-drivers' battalion during the First World War. As a politician, he had risen under the shadow of the British Empire and its mighty armed forces. He distrusted Hagana's 'partisan' officers, claiming that 'our men, though good Zionists, have not yet learnt how to fight'. Having already received Yadin's report, he summoned Dayan and had him retell the story. Though impressed, he told Dayan it had been a one-time success; this, he said, 'is no way to wage a war'.[32] The assessment did not interfere with his decision to appoint Dayan to command the Jerusalem Brigade, which had been made as early as 29 June. Nor did he alter it when a delegation from 89th Battalion asked him to leave their commander with them.

Ben Gurion's real motives in promoting the scarcely known major to one of the most important posts in the army will never be known. He adamantly refused to accept Allon who was the candidate of Yadin and the General Staff; to some extent, insisting on Dayan was a way of showing who was boss. Probably what Ben Gurion really wanted was somebody who did not have a political party behind him, as many did, PALMACH officers in particular; and who, in spite of his reputation as a fire-eating hawk, had a record of unconditional obedience in implementing even the most unwelcome orders. For Dayan, the decision meant that he would henceforward operate directly under the Prime Minister's eye in one of the world's most disputed trouble spots.

On the night of 17/18 July Dayan had a last fling in the role he liked best, i.e. that of a modern-day cavalry commander. Turning his efforts against the Egyptians, he and his men charged an outpost on the eastern extremity of the front in order to roll it up and bring about its collapse. Proceeding at night – hardly the best time for a motorized battalion – the advance was as wild and unorganized as the attack on Lydda and Ramle had been. At one point the column of vehicles got stuck, under fire, in a wadi from which there was no exit. Having found the right man to dig them out Dayan, who was exhausted and at that moment had nothing better to do, took a nap; as Bismarck once put it, a king *must* sleep. His ability to do so at the right time impressed his men and restored confidence. Having stormed the position he handed it over to another unit and departed, leaving his successors to cope with a fierce Egyptian counter-attack. Later there was talk of court-martialling Dayan for having acted without orders. In so far as the charges against him were dropped, though, he was vindicated.

Carrying the insignia of a lieutenant colonel on his shoulders, Dayan went to Jerusalem. At the time it was a city of about 100,000 (counting Jews only), desolate from four months of fighting. Its eastern half, including the Old City and the Holy Places, were in Jordanian hands. The streets were cratered and many buildings carried the marks of shells and bullets; people drank rainwater and looked for wild plants in the fields to supplement their diet. Reunited after months of separation, the Dayan family lived in a huge villa that had once housed Ethiopian emperor Haile Selassie during his exile. Never before had they occupied a residence with more than two rooms. Though coming under occasional fire, they soon began to share it with others, politicians, officers and diplomats, who lived in different parts of the building or drifted in and out, creating a busy social life such as he and Ruth had never had before.

Not long after his arrival in Jerusalem Dayan launched two small attacks on outlying neighbourhoods under Jordanian control. However, the local troops were not up to par and the attacks were beaten back. One area they failed to take was the height of Nebi Samuel where the legion had stationed its artillery; another was Beth Jalla, the suburb of Bethlehem from where, fifty years later, Palestinian fighters were to fire at Jewish Jerusalem. In the meantime, the nature of his mission changed. Originally Ben Gurion had contemplated the reconquest of the entire

West Bank from the Jordanians who were holding it. As the summer of 1948 turned into autumn, however, he became increasingly inclined to accept the existing lines as permanent borders including, as a necessary if very painful part of this, the division of Jerusalem. On his instructions Dayan became involved in negotiations with his Jordanian opposite number, Abdullah el Tel, with the objective of settling the details in his sector.

Like many Jordanian officers, Tel was strongly anti-British. More important, both his superiors and those of Dayan objected to the UN's plan of November 1947 under which Jerusalem would come under international control. Amidst much manoeuvring, these shared interests created a bond between them, until they were finally able to deal with each other without the need for UN mediation. Paradoxically, the telephone line that linked them sealed the partition of Jerusalem between Arabs and Jews; at the same time, it served to exclude anyone else. Dayan's skills as a diplomat were appreciated. He took part in the armistice talks that were held in Rhodes at the beginning of 1949. On three occasions he was selected to accompany Foreign Minister Moshe Sharet on missions to King Abdullah; his role in these negotiations was to play the hawk to Sharet's dove. Years later, Ben Gurion praised Dayan for securing the railway that linked Jerusalem to Tel Aviv, as well as another slice of the West Bank, for Israel. The Prime Minister was a tough and vindictive character who was not above rewriting history if doing so suited his ends. Probably his real motive in giving credit to Dayan was to deny it to the more senior negotiators, particularly Sharet, whom he saw as a possible competitor for his own position. Needless to say, neither Sharet nor the members of his staff saw Dayan's role in quite the same light.

During the period covered in this chapter the Jewish armed forces in the land of Israel grew from a few dozen irregulars to an army numbering 90,000 men and women complete with twelve brigades, some armour, an embryonic navy and air force, and even a 'psychological service'. Yet almost all of this had been accomplished under British rule; meaning that they had to operate more or less underground, and were unable either to organize, train, or arm properly. Instead they had to be content with small-scale operations under the watchful eye of their British overlords; who, as Dayan's own career showed, made use of them when needed but kept them on a tight leash when not. Within days of emerging from underground, still unorganized and with practically no heavy weapons, they were confronted by five invading regular armies. There was no choice but to fight or die. Fight they did, and 6,000 Israelis, almost 1 per cent of the population, did die. Of the members of PALMACH, which bore the brunt of the fighting at Degania among other places, the number killed in action reached 20 per cent. A real *kindermord* (slaughter of the innocents), to borrow the First World War German expression.

Joining Hagana when it was just emerging from infancy, Dayan had grown up with it. Partly because of his injury, partly because he did not belong to any group or clique, he was neither the most rapidly promoted commander nor the most successful one. By the time the war ended he was still only a colonel; the largest force he had commanded in battle was a battalion. When it came to sheer hard fighting, though, he was second to none. As the operation against Lydda and Ramle showed, he was already developing the qualities that were to stand him in good stead, such as guile, speed and flexibility, as well as determination and ruthlessness. More important still, combat was the medium that made him come to life. Years later he called it the most exciting thing in the world; immediately adding that the excitement it offered was no reason for engaging in it. Men followed him partly because he looked after them and partly because of his charm. Visiting two subordinates who had been wounded in the eye he told them one eye was enough to see all there was in this lousy world.[33] When all else failed, his contempt for death shamed them into doing as he did.

Had this been all, Dayan might have earned a minor place in history as a fighting commander. He was indeed a fighting commander; but already at this stage he was also the most prominent commander among the politicians and the most prominent politician among the commanders. Somehow an appearance of frankness went hand in hand with a capacity for behind the scenes manoeuvring, intrigue and skullduggery. Fierce independence combined with a willingness to implement even the most unpalatable orders – including the partition of Jerusalem, the most unpalatable of all. Whether because he was captivated by Dayan's personality or because he found the young commander a useful tool against his party competitors, Ben Gurion supported him, and it was his support that mattered. Dayan, in turn, came to see the Prime Minister as the only person to whose judgement he was prepared to defer. From then on, for many years, they were to march together.

CHAPTER 3

Top Gun

In October 1949 Dayan's promotion to brigadier general and his appointment as Commanding Officer, Southern Front, marked his arrival as one of the top officers in the Israeli Army. His predecessor had been Yigal Allon. In the 1948 War Allon had been the most successful Israeli commander by far, fighting first in the north, then in the centre, and finally in the south. There, he crowned his achievements by decisively defeating the Egyptian invaders and driving them back into the Sinai; had Ben Gurion not held him back at the last moment, he would have annihilated them. However, like his former superior Sadeh, Allon was politically suspect and was driven out of the service by Ben Gurion, a blow from which his career never recovered. Upon his arrival Dayan retained Allon's entire team. The one exception was Yitzhak Rabin, for whom he had 'no use'.[34] The dislike was mutual; writing to Allon, who had been packed off to study at Oxford, Rabin said that 'Moshe D. has arrived. I show him around. The fellow knows nothing about anything. I think he lacks any understanding of military affairs above company or battalion level. Besides, he is completely without tact'.[35] In fact, no two officers could be more different than the clear-headed, methodical, pedestrian Rabin and the 'wild', intuitive, charismatic Dayan. Luckily for Rabin he was able to obtain a post in the training branch; for which, as it turned out, he was ideally suited.

The Negev, where Dayan was now based, was the largest and most important of the IDF's territorial commands. Though bare and almost entirely unpopulated, the desert had a harsh beauty of its own; many years later he still rhapsodized about the 'wide-open, hot, dry, and awe-inspiring vistas'[36] that now opened themselves to him. Sometimes taking his daughter along, his first step was to familiarize himself with it by way of extensive trips during which they would sleep in the open. Since the border was still unmarked, those trips were not entirely safe, at least once they strayed beyond it. In a typical display of nerve, Dayan's reaction was to convince the local Egyptian commander that *he* had strayed. By the time the confusion was sorted out and the Egyptians sent up fighter aircraft to take care of the intruders, Dayan and his party were gone.

In his memoirs Dayan calls the period uneventful, emphasizing the help which, at Ben Gurion's orders, Southern Command gave to the new Jewish settlements then being built in the area. In fact there were countless skirmishes with smugglers, Bedouin, and refugees who were trying to return to the land they had lost in 1948. The Bedouin and refugees he expelled, gathering them up, confiscating much of their property, loading them on lorries and forcing them across the border with Jordan or the Gaza Strip by firing over their heads if necessary. Then as always, he felt that what had to be done had to be done. At one MAPAI meeting – the line between politics and the military was not yet as strict as it should have been – he expressed the hope that Israel might yet have an opportunity to 'transfer' its remaining 170,000 Arabs.[37]

Another episode left unmentioned is the manoeuvres of 1951 when he commanded an 'Egyptian' invasion. He and his men set up well-integrated fighting teams. They dispensed with complicated pre-battle procedures, achieved surprise, drove their vehicles across the fields instead of over the highways, and, bypassing the crossroads together with the umpires stationed at them, went straight for the defenders' jugular. Dayan contributed to the deception by positioning himself with a phantom force whose mission was to carry out a feint. He won a smashing victory, deciding the exercise before it had even begun and messing it up to such an extent that many of its objectives could not be accomplished. Predictably, his superiors told him that breaking the rules was no great feat – in which, since he had ignored logistics, they had right on their side. Typically, he answered that doing so was just what war is all about; as to the logistics, they would take care of themselves after the victory.[38]

Amidst all this, he was aware of how limited his military education was – his former deputy, Peltz, claimed he did not even know how to read a map – and developed a thirst for knowledge. First, though already a brigadier general, he took part in a course for battalion commanders. The head of the course was Haim Laskov. The way Dayan saw things, the instructors focused too much on operations, while ignoring political realities such as the impossibility of abandoning Jewish settlements in front of an advancing enemy; nor was he a man to conceal his views. For the graduation ceremony he produced a caricature in which he compared the instructors to wise owls and himself to a crafty fox who had come to steal from them. Next he was sent to study with the British Army, attending a three-month senior commanders' course. Nobody had to teach him how to fight, and administrative details always bored him to tears. Nevertheless, for the first time in his life he was made to put his decisions down in writing and justify them. To this extent the course was useful to him; had it depended on him, he would have stayed in England for longer and studied more.

After six more months as Commanding Officer, Northern Front, Dayan was made chief of the General Staff Division of the General Staff, a position second only to that of chief of staff, General Mordechai Maklef. The latter had wanted Rabin but was overruled by Ben Gurion, who had no intention of forgetting Rabin's link with Allon and thus to Ben Gurion's political rivals to the left. This complicated mating dance goes some way to explain the events that followed. The Israeli staff system of the time resembled the British one, which in turn had been copied from the Germans. Its ostensible purpose was to relieve the chief of staff of administrative detail, but Dayan, with Ben Gurion behind him, was able to reverse the roles by disappearing on impromptu visits to units and installations so that, paradoxically, it was Maklef who was saddled with running the army day to day. The system, if that is the right term, left him plenty of time to read the raw intelligence reports that he preferred. It also enabled him to see people – even at short notice – and to think; every few months he would gather his thoughts in a lecture to his men.

He gave his subordinates plenty of elbow room, consulting with them, taking their advice, and making sure they did not simply waste their time on unnecessary tasks. Several are on record as saying he was the best schoolmaster they ever had; typically, he once told some of them that their task was to put right in the afternoon what he had done wrong in the morning.[39] So long as one retained his trust, working for him was much easier than commanding him. Once trust had been broken there were no half measures and, perhaps because he had seen Ben Gurion in action, he could be almost as brutal towards subordinates as towards the enemy. His leisure occupations included shooting pigeons – he found his salary insufficient and they supplemented the family diet – and archaeology. The latter was soon to become a passion, until no site, however insignificant, was safe from his roving eye and sharp spade.

Dayan's tenure as *de facto* second in command only lasted from 7 December 1952 to 6 December 1953, but was extremely eventful. This was the period when border incidents were becoming more and more serious as parties of 'infiltrators' crossed into Israel from the neighbouring countries to rob, demolish, kill, mutilate and occasionally also rape. Typically, Dayan did not join those who formulated elaborate condemnations of the perpetrators; to him they were always simply poor devils trying to avenge their defeat and/or regain some of what had they had lost in war. When invited to give funeral speeches he used these to condemn those Israelis who had failed to keep their eyes open and their weapons sharp. He demanded harsh retaliatory measures in such cases – 'not because they are moral, but because they are effective'.[40]

In fact harsh retaliatory measures were taken, but were not effective. Time after time during the first half of 1953 the IDF launched punitive expeditions, mainly across the border with Jordan. Time after time they failed to reach their objective, revealing poor preparation, poor skills in such fields as navigation and marksmanship, and, above all, poor motivation. These problems affected not just individual units but the entire army. One reason for this was Ben Gurion's policy of discharging ex-PALMACH officers, which led to the loss of many of the best commanders. Other reasons included the enlisting of so many immigrants from so many countries that mobilization orders had to be read in thirteen different languages, as well as a manpower system which placed the best-educated recruits in support units instead of in the combat arms.

As Winston Churchill once wrote, war can be made either by butchery or by guile. For Dayan, guile had always been supremely important – it was not for nothing that he drew himself as a fox – but unlike some others he never thought it could, or indeed should, substitute for butchery. His immediate response to the problem now facing the IDF was a series of lectures to commanders as well as new standing orders. In them he demanded that they abandon 'Jewish cleverness' and put the objective first; those who abandoned an attack before at least 50 per cent of their men had become casualties would be called to account. The figure of 50 per cent was probably exaggerated, since few forces in history have fought that hard. Still the doctrine behind it was sound; from then until the 1982 invasion of Lebanon began to sap its powers, 'maintenance of aim' became the overriding principle on which the IDF operated. At the time, however, mere words – even words coming from a commander famous for his courage – were not enough, and Maklef cast about for other methods.

In the event, Dayan's idea of combining guile *and* butchery was destined to be put into practice by a new unit, No. 101, and its commander, the then Major Ariel Sharon. Dayan himself had originally opposed its creation, arguing that the entire army needed to be shaken up and that Sharon's force would obstruct that objective by attracting the best personnel. Later, having realized that Sharon and his men were turning into a model for the entire army to follow, he was to change his view; another proof of a willingness to learn that was one of his chief strengths. In October 1953, after infiltrators had thrown a hand grenade into a house at Yahud (not far from Tel Aviv) killing a woman and two of her children, Sharon, along with twenty of his volunteers and another force of paratroopers, carried out the first major reprisal. They crossed the border into Jordan, overpowered the watchmen at the village of Kibiye, and blew up fifty houses complete with the seventy people in them. Later Sharon claimed he had thought the houses were empty. To deflect the storm of criticism that followed, Ben Gurion felt forced to tell the world that the action had been carried out by private individuals and not by the IDF, none of whose units, he claimed, had left base.

By that time Ben Gurion was on his way out, having delegated his portfolio as Minister of Defence to a veteran MAPAI politician, Pinhas Lavon. In December 1953 he also surrendered his post as Prime Minister, this time to Moshe Sharet; as his last act in office, he replaced the chief of staff, Maklef, with Dayan. Wittingly or unwittingly – probably the former – he thereby created an explosive mixture of clashing personalities. Dayan was a confirmed hawk or 'activist', as the Israeli phrase went. He always insisted that only blows could answer blows and, perhaps, put an end to them; once he said that to survive amidst 40 million Arabs, Israel had to behave like 'a rabid dog that nobody dares to touch'.[41] By contrast, Sharet had risen by way of the Foreign Service and was first and foremost a diplomat. He was proud of his knowledge of Arab culture, hoping to use it to build bridges between Israel and its neighbours; Dayan he saw as a dangerous hothead. Finally, Lavon had long been known as a dove, having opposed the measures ordered by Ben Gurion – and implemented by Dayan among others – to expel Arabs from Israeli territory. Once in office, he suddenly changed his feathers and became almost as hawkish as his main subordinate, proposing, as Sharet confided to his diary, 'the satanic doctrine of setting the Middle East on fire, stirring up war, organizing bloody coups, striking targets belonging to the Powers, desperate and suicidal acts'.[42]

The atrocity at Kibiye caused the emphasis to shift from civilian to military targets – Israel's declared policy was now to blame the Jordanian authorities for failing to stop the terrorists – but it did not change the policy of retaliation. Sharon's command was expanded until it comprised an entire battalion of paratroopers, who rained blows upon the hapless Jordanians. On their return they would find Dayan waiting for them with a supply of alcoholic drinks. The chief of staff wanted to learn everything he could at first hand; his realization that knowledge is power had always been one of his strengths. Repeatedly Sharet, who had to explain Sharon's actions to the world, was surprised by the size of the raids. Repeatedly Lavon and Dayan explained that 'operational complications' had caused the number of Jordanian – and sometimes Israeli – casualties to be far greater than anticipated. When it came to misleading Sharet – the Prime Minister was not even told of reconnaissance operations conducted in enemy territory – Lavon could count on Dayan and Dayan could count on Sharon. Much later, Sharon himself wrote that Dayan's reason for preferring him was precisely because he never asked for written orders.[43]

Another major concern of the same year, 1954, was the so-called 'Affair'. In a misguided attempt to prevent the British from evacuating Egypt, an Israeli intelligence team in that country was activated and its members ordered to place a number of small bombs in British and American targets. Little damage was done, but the team leader betrayed his subordinates to the Egyptian authorities, causing them to be arrested. They were put on trial and two were executed; in Israel, the debacle led to a fierce debate as to who had given 'the instruction' for the operation to go ahead. The evidence pointed to the chief of military intelligence, Colonel Benjamin Gibli. Gibli claimed he had received the order directly from Lavon, who denied any knowledge. The 'Affair' kept Israeli politics busy for years as charges, counter-charges and committees of investigation followed each other. As Gibli's direct superior, Dayan was at least as hawkish as his own direct superior, Lavon. He was well aware of the existence of the unit that had carried out the operation; contrary to what he and his supporters later claimed, too, at the time when the first explosion took place – 2 July – he was still in Israel and not in the USA. All this provides an excellent example of his unerring ability to avoid responsibility. On one occasion a subordinate asked him whether a 'don't take prisoners' order meant that those prisoners had to be killed or released. 'I leave that to you' was the answer he received.[44]

The aftermath of the 'Affair' forced Lavon to resign, Ben Gurion being brought back as Minister of Defence in February 1955. Linked to Dayan by a common 'activist' approach to security policy as well as mutual admiration, Ben Gurion and Dayan intrigued together behind Sharet's back. In the hope of getting the West as well as the United Nations on Israel's side, Sharet tried to ignore terrorist attacks as far as possible.

Some attacks, though, were too brutal even for him. Reluctantly, he would agree to a retaliatory strike with an estimate of, say, ten Arab dead, only to wake up next morning to discover that Sharon and his men had not only killed forty but had also blown up an entire base. From the spring of 1955 on, the strikes were increasingly directed against the Egyptians rather than the Jordanians. In part, this was because Ben Gurion and Dayan wanted to put an end to ongoing international attempts to achieve peace between Egypt and Israel at the cost, to the latter, of surrendering a strip of territory in the Negev Desert. In part, it was because Palestinian terrorists were using the Gaza Strip as a springboard for actions against Israel. Some of their actions were authorized by the Egyptians, others not. Later Egyptian Intelligence itself took a hand, establishing units of *Fedayeen* – those who sacrifice themselves – to infiltrate, spy, and kill.

In approving the raids, Ben Gurion and Dayan hoped to teach Colonel Gamal Abdul Nasser, who had taken over as Egypt's ruler two years earlier, a lesson. What they achieved was the exact opposite. Rather than rein in the *Fedayeen*, Nasser turned to the Soviets and signed an arms deal with them; nor was this to be the last time that Israel misjudged his intentions, causing him to escalate the conflict instead of giving way. The deal, which was revealed to the world in August 1955, included 90–100 modern jet fighters, 48 light jet bombers, 230 tanks, destroyers, submarines, and torpedo boats; this, at a time when Israel itself only had 50 obsolescent jet fighters and a total of 130 tanks, mostly of Second World War vintage. Shortly after the deal was concluded, Nasser added fuel to the flames by closing the Straits of Tyran to Israeli shipping. In panic, Israeli public opinion blamed Sharet. In November he returned to his old post as Foreign Minister, leaving that of Prime Minister to Ben Gurion.

By this time Dayan, having been in office for about a year, was running the IDF with a strong hand. Every three weeks or so he called a meeting of the General Staff. Usually there were about ten people present; sometimes there were guests, particularly the 32-year-old director of the Ministry of Defence, Shimon Peres. Most meetings lasted for about two hours and, in so far as participants addressed each other by their nicknames, were of a relatively informal character. Issues discussed ranged from cuts in manpower – Dayan hoped to save money for acquisition – to an extra $5 a month that officers were supposed to receive as an allowance for running their vehicles; and from 'administrative discipline' to the need to convert infantry weapons to a different type of ammunition. Dayan always delivered the opening statement himself and always summed up. Often he got involved in detail – for example, in discussing the question of whether or not IDF personnel should wear ties (they still don't) and, if so, under what circumstances. He had developed a characteristic way of talking that combined directness with a literary quality rare among his colleagues. (As I skimmed the records, I was soon able to recognize his style even without looking to see who was saying what.)

Throughout all this, Dayan remained his usual hawkish self. True, the retaliatory strikes he organized against Nasser and others – in December 1955 there was a particularly vicious one against the Syrians, with Sharon commanding once again – had failed to cow the Egyptian leader. In the meantime, though, his policy of raising the IDF's fighting spirit was beginning to bear fruit. Other units, jealous of the paratroopers and looking for a share in the glory, were clamouring to be given missions similar to theirs. In years to come Israel's fighting power, which had reached its nadir at about the time Dayan entered office as chief of the General Staff Division, was to become almost legendary; he himself was identified with it, not without reason. He encouraged it by every means at his disposal, visiting units, deliberately causing them to compete with each other, making them feel proud of their achievements and ensuring that their exploits were presented by the media in the most favourable light possible.

During his term as chief of the General Staff Division Dayan had brought in a staff officer, Colonel Yuval Neeman (later a world-famous nuclear scientist), as head of the planning branch. Neeman's task was to prepare contingency plans for large-scale offensive warfare against all of Israel's neighbours; had those plans been carried out, the IDF would have overrun not just the territories taken in 1967 but Amman, Damascus, Tripoli in Lebanon and even the Saudi oilfields. Later, Dayan explicitly told Ben Gurion that one objective behind the increasingly violent retaliatory strikes was to 'escalate'[45] the situation. The Egyptians, he reasoned, needed time to absorb the new weapons; hence the longer Israel delayed its attack the more casualties it would suffer. By the spring of 1956 at the latest, the General Staff, on Dayan's orders, was also preparing much more detailed plans for the occupation of the Gaza Strip and the Straits of Tyran. Still it was Ben Gurion, not he, who had to bear the ultimate responsibility. The Prime Minister had his doubts. In part, these were due to the fact that Israel had failed to obtain arms from the USA. In part, these originated in his fears that a full-scale offensive against Egypt might lead to an angry response on the part of 'the Powers', some of which, he believed, might go so far as to bombard Israel's own cities.

In the event, the first of these concerns was destined to be alleviated by another one of Ben Gurion's protégés, Shimon Peres. During the period in question he had not yet discovered that his real mission in life was battling for peace. Instead he was considered very much a hawk among hawks, albeit one whose real talents lay in administration and diplomacy rather than in soldiering. In turn, France's willingness to provide Israel with arms was a direct outcome of the Algerian Revolt which had broken out in 1953 and which was soon to keep no fewer than 400,000 French troops occupied. The way Paris saw it, the Israeli Army, in its strikes against the Egyptians and Syria, had given impressive proof of its capabilities as well as its high fighting morale; behind the IDF, Israel itself was beginning to feel as if fighting was its great mission in life. Now the two sides drew closely together, even to the point where the Israelis agreed to act as contractors for their allies and engage in assassination attempts in several Arab capitals.

Had the Israelis and the French been left on their own, the Suez Campaign would never have been fought. As it was, an opportunity for drawing in Great Britain was provided by Nasser's decision of 20 July 1956 to nationalize the Suez Canal. With not one but two Western powers on Israel's side, Ben Gurion felt he could launch the attack against Egypt. The problem was that the French would not move without the British; whereas the latter needed an excuse to satisfy domestic public opinion. Talks at creating the alliance, which on the Israeli side were conducted mainly by Peres and members of the General Staff, went on throughout the summer and autumn, culminating at a tripartite meeting held at Sèvres on 23–24 October 1956. In the end it was the French General Challe who came up with the formula the British needed. Under its terms Israel would open the campaign by attacking, or pretending to attack, the Suez Canal. Claiming the need to keep it open for shipping, France and Britain would put an ultimatum for both Israel and the Egyptians to withdraw from the area. Egypt would refuse, providing the Western powers with a pretext for the intervention to follow.

Dayan's role in all this was critical. Since at least the middle of 1955 he had been nudging his superior in the direction of war. Now, at Sèvres, he found that the Prime Minister had still not been entirely convinced. Not without reason, Ben Gurion understood the plan as a British plot to make Israel take the blame for the aggression. Besides, he was concerned that the Western powers might not keep to their part of the bargain; should they renege, he was afraid, having spent some time in

London during the Blitz, that a similar fate might overtake Tel Aviv. It took all of the chief of staff's powers of persuasion to bring the parties together and make his superior change his mind. First, the French agreed to station several air force squadrons in Israel and send two destroyers to cover Israel's long coast. Second, the ultimatum to be addressed to Israel – but not to Egypt – was changed into a 'request'. Third, and most important, Dayan was able to persuade Ben Gurion that, should France and Britain fail to live up to their promises, then the Israeli action could be presented as another retaliatory strike. The force responsible for it would simply be withdrawn; in this way no great harm would be done. In the end, agreement was reached. That evening he and some junior staff-members went out to a nightclub. As he later wrote, however, not even 'the most curvaceous strip-teasers in Paris'[46] could divert his mind from the task ahead.

It was time to make the final preparations. From July on, dozens of modern French jet fighters and as many as three hundred tanks were unloaded on Israel's shores, first in secret and then openly. To these were added anti-tank missiles and 6x6 trucks vital for desert operations; the total cost was $80 million, which was about equal to the annual defence budget in each of the years 1953–55. Almost overnight, what had hitherto been mainly an infantry force had turned into an armour-heavy one, with all that such a change implies in respect to organization, training, logistics, doctrine and the like.

To accomplish the change Dayan turned to Laskov, who was head of the General Staff Division, and appointed him to head the armoured corps that had been established in the previous year. Laskov, who owed his previous post to Ben Gurion's insistence, was as straightforward as Dayan was evasive and wily. He took his transfer as a calculated insult; which it may well have been. It was only after Ben Gurion intervened personally and promised him that his new post would by no means compromise his chances of succeeding Dayan that he set to work. He proved to be the right man for the job. By the time the campaign opened the IDF had three fairly battle-worthy armoured brigades, though the equipment of one of them left much to be desired. The problem was that Dayan had hardly any experience with tanks and did not understand what they could do. Instead of using them to spearhead the attack, he wanted them to provide fire support for the kind of mechanized infantry battalion he himself had commanded in 1948. At one point he even suggested that they be brought up on trucks.

On 3 October, the General Staff was told that war was about to break out and operational planning started. The IDF could put about 45,000 men into the campaign. Meanwhile the Egyptian Army, largely because they were anticipating a possible Anglo-French landing, the preparations for which could not be concealed, had only 30,000 men in the Sinai; of those, about a third were second-rate National Guard and Palestinian troops. The bulk of these forces were concentrated in the strongly fortified areas around Rafah and Abu Agheila, each of which commanded one of the two key roads running east to west; standing in reserve at El Arish was one brigade. To the south of Abu Agheila, where the topography is much more difficult, there were only company-sized forces. The defensive array – and defensive it clearly was – was completed by two battalions at the far southern end of the peninsula, covering the straits.

Early on, Israeli planning had assumed that the IDF would strike at the Gaza Strip, the Straits of Tyran, or both; now, following the Sèvres agreement, it became necessary to proceed from west to east in order to introduce a force near the Suez Canal first of all. The change also meant that the air force had to be put on a leash. Its original intention had been to concentrate on the Egyptian airfields and to smash the enemy on the ground, in preparation for a Blitzkrieg campaign such as the Germans might have launched in the Second World War. Instead, it had to be content with protecting friendly airspace as well as supporting the land operations. The task of taking care of the Egyptian Air Force was left to the British and the French. Using Cyprus as their base, the allies were to open their own offensive thirty-six hours after the IDF first crossed the border.

The final Israeli plan provided for a battalion of paratroopers to be landed near the Parker Memorial, east of the Mitla Pass and about 30 miles from the Suez Canal. The next step was to link up with the paratroopers and create a land corridor; this was the task of Ariel Sharon and the other two paratrooper battalions he now commanded. The IDF's main forces, organized into two *ugdas*, or divisions, and comprising seven brigades, were only to go into action after the French and the British fulfilled their part of the bargain and attacked Egypt in turn. First 38th *ugda* was to attack the main Egyptian fortified area at Abu Agheila in the centre of Sinai, then 77th *ugda* was to assault the fortifications of Rafah further north. Thus, the Israeli offensive would proceed in echelon with the southern wing leading; only after everything else was complete would an independent brigade move from Elath along the Red Sea shore in order to occupy the Straits of Tyran. In Dayan's own words, the highly original plan was intended to bring about the 'collapse' of the Egyptian forces, capture their equipment and overrun the Sinai. Killing as many enemy troops as possible was not one of its aims.

While everything in the plan depended on surprise, the mobilization of over 100,000 reservists could not be concealed. In this respect, and a critically important one it was, events assisted Israel and Dayan. During 1955 and the first half of 1956 the border with Jordan had been relatively quiet. In September 1956, however, it flared up again as an Israeli unit in training crossed into Jordanian territory – by mistake, says Dayan – and started off another round of raids, infiltrations and retaliatory strikes. The heaviest strike of all, launched in response to the assassination of two Israeli civilians not far from Tel Aviv, took place at Kalkilya, on Israel's narrow 'waist', on the night of 10/11 October. As was standard practice during this period, the target was a police station held by the Arab Legion. As was also standard practice at this time, another force was sent out further to the east in order to ambush Jordanian reinforcements. However, the plan went wrong. Returning to base, the ambushers ran into an ambush; to get his men out, Dayan had to activate the Israeli Air Force. By the time the operation ended, about 80 Jordanian and 17 Israeli soldiers lay dead, with 68 other Israelis wounded and hospitalized.

As Dayan wrote,[47] the policy of retaliatory strikes, which he himself had done so much to establish, had reached the end of the road. The Jordanians, however, did not know this, and Dayan made the best possible use of that fact. Sharon's force, which had carried out all previous strikes, and whose task was to carry out the second move in the campaign after the initial paratrooper landings, was concentrated on Israel's eastern frontier. Dayan was thus playing on Jordanian fears; at the same time, he concealed the real objective from the Egyptians on Israel's opposite side. After the war started and the paratroopers landed at the Mitla, Sharon crossed Israel from east to west before driving into the Sinai. The movement added about twelve hours to the time he needed to reach the Mitla, a risk that Dayan, trusting to his paratroopers' fighting prowess and to the air force's ability to intervene in the ground battle, was ready to take. Surveying the final preparations, Laskov, who as we saw had no reason to like Dayan, was moved to pen a note praising his superior's 'marvellous leadership'.[48] In the end he did not send it; but only because he feared it might be interpreted in the wrong way.

The main moves of the Suez Campaign have been described many times and need not be repeated here. Instead we shall try to follow them as Dayan himself experienced them, step by step. He spent the final hours before H-hour writing and rewriting the IDF's press release that was to accompany the descent of the paratroopers near the Mitla Pass. This he brought to Ben Gurion who, as was often the case during moments of extreme tension, had taken to his bed with a high fever and was suffering from last-minute jitters. He asked the chief of staff why Israel was going to war later that day: 'Because it will be five o'clock' (i.e. H-hour), was Dayan's reply. Having obtained the Prime Minister's reluctant blessing, Dayan hurried back to General Headquarters. He found his subordinates in high spirits, happy because they were going to teach Nasser a lesson and doubly happy at finally being able to put into practice what they had been preparing for for years. He himself did not share their elation. This was not because he had any last-minute reservations. On the contrary, as he later wrote, it was because he knew the campaign might still have to be aborted should Britain and France fail to carry out their part in the common plan.

The night of 29/30 October was spent at General Headquarters receiving reports that came in from the paratroopers as well as the air force. On the whole, the feeling was one of relief; things had gone according to plan, more or less, and fears lest the Egyptians send a large number of aircraft to bomb Israel had not materialized. Early on the morning of 30 October Dayan drove to Kusseima, a small Egyptian outpost south of Abu Agheila, which had just been taken by 4th Infantry Brigade. Since the campaign might still have to be suspended, it had been his intention to halt the forces at Kusseima and reorganize. He was astonished to learn that the Commanding Officer, Southern Front, General Asaf Simhoni, had violated his orders and thrown in his main force – 7th Armoured Brigade – forty-eight hours earlier than expected.

A furious argument followed. Dayan yelled at Simhoni for ignoring his orders, and the latter answered that keeping the armour in reserve instead of throwing it in at the outset was such a bad error that it could not be tolerated – a view he reiterated to Ben Gurion after the war, shortly before he was killed when the aircraft in which he was travelling was shot down. At the time, all Dayan could do was to chase 7th Armoured in the hope of halting it before it was able to advance too far; catching up with it, however, he found the time had already passed. Like a good chessplayer he made the best of a bad job. First he ordered the commander of 7th Armoured, a Colonel Uri Ben Ari, to outflank the main Egyptian fortifications at Abu Agheila from the south. Next, having returned to Kusseima, he ordered *ugda* headquarters to use its two other brigades – 10th Infantry and 37th Armoured – to attack those fortifications on the same evening, twenty-four hours earlier than planned. On his way back to Israel, to his surprised delight, he discovered lying in the sand some arrowheads and other stone tools dating back 6,000–8,000 years.

Having spent most of the day driving to and fro in the desert, that evening he returned to Tel Aviv and visited GHQ, before going to see Ben Gurion who was still in bed. From him he learnt that the British and French had postponed the beginning of their attack by another day. This made the advance of 7th Armoured Brigade, and with it the attack on the fortifications at Abu Agheila, even more problematic than it already was; he did not even dare tell the news to Ben Gurion. Returning to the Sinai, he was determined to push the attack on that area at all costs in order not to leave 7th Armoured hanging out on a limb. Partly because of his own contradictory orders, partly because his travels caused him to lose touch with GHQ – which was trying to sort out the mess but was unable to find him – the attack did not proceed as fast as he would have wished. The first attempts were repulsed with bloody losses that included part of a brigade headquarters; in the end the Egyptians, acting on their own initiative and not because they were pressed, evacuated Abu Agheila during the night of 31 October/1 November. Though he did recognize

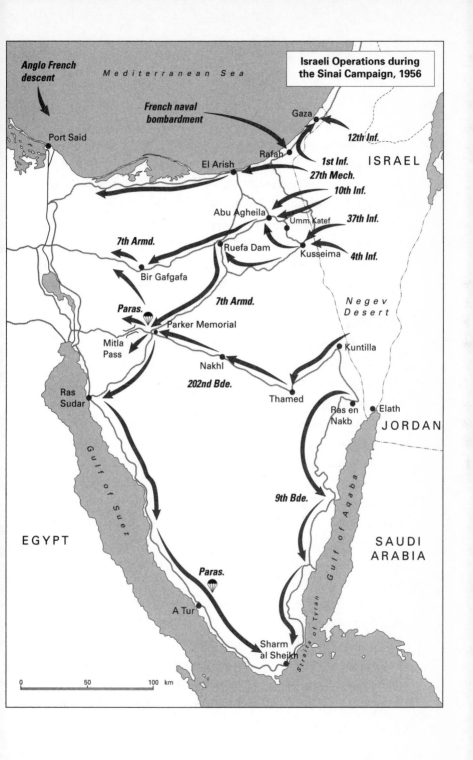

his own part in the failure, Dayan was not amused and not long after he fired the divisional commander as well as two brigade commanders.

His staff, made wise by experience, would have liked Dayan to stay at GHQ, but he refused, claiming he had no choice. The evening of 31 October found him at the headquarters of 77th *ugda*, whose commander was Laskov, its task being to break through the powerful Egyptian fortifications at Rafah. Dayan spent the whole of the 1 November with Laskov's spearhead, which consisted of 27th Armoured Brigade, under the command of Colonel Haim Bar Lev. They came under occasional fire from Egyptian stragglers, and Dayan's radio operator was killed right beside him. The town of El Arish, which is the largest in the Sinai, fell early on the 2nd after the local Egyptian brigade left it without a fight. While 27th Armoured continued west, Dayan spent a couple of spare hours in the area looking for antiques. Mission accomplished, at 1100 hours he boarded a light aircraft and flew back to Tel Aviv.

By this time Ben Gurion had recovered and was in an excellent, even elated, mood. Dayan gave his report and spent the evening at GHQ. Early the next morning a message arrived from the commander of 9th Brigade whose advance along the shore of the Red Sea was being held up by the extremely difficult terrain. Consulting his staff – for once, he was there to tell them what to do – Dayan decided to assist the attack on the straits by using one of the three battalions of paratroopers at the Mitla. Its mission was to reach A Tur, on the Gulf of Suez, by land and capture the local airstrip. Next, transport aircraft would land another battalion there. Of the combined force, two companies were to be airlifted to the straits and descend by parachute. The rest were supposed to drive down the south-western shore of the peninsula in order to reach the straits from the opposite direction from that of 9th Brigade, and turn the assault on the Egyptian positions into a two-armed one.

Late on the night of 2/3 November Dayan boarded a transport aircraft and flew to see the situation of 9th Brigade at first hand. The terrain made it impossible for them to land, and he had to content himself by radioing the brigade commander. They flew right across the Sinai and, early on the morning of 3 November, landed at A Tur, which was now in Israeli hands. Another discussion led to the decision to cancel the planned parachute drop near the straits; the wind was too strong, and the operation too dangerous. Instead, the entire force was to proceed by road. They took off again, landing first at the Mitla, then at Bir Hama in the centre of the Sinai (where Dayan met with the commander of 7th Brigade), then finally at El Arish where he discussed the arrangements for setting up a military government. By 1900 hours they were back in Israel.

At 0800 hours on the 4th he held a staff meeting at GHQ. Though the British and the French had not even started their promised landing at Port Said, with the exception of the straits and a strip along the canal the entire peninsula was now in Israeli hands; it was, indeed, already becoming possible to consider the discharge of some reservists. In the afternoon he drove to Gaza, only 50 or so miles south of Tel Aviv, where it was necessary to make arrangements for governing the Strip's population of 180,000. Here too he found time to engage in a little archaeological digging, uncovering a grave and deciding – he was already becoming something of an expert – that it dated to about 1300 BC.

In the evening, since 9th Brigade had not yet captured the straits, he decided to revisit A Tur the next day in order to fly from there south-wards. Landing the transport aircraft at the little airstrip he found that somebody had misunderstood his orders and that no light aircraft was waiting to take them on the next leg of the trip; he and his party com-mandeered some Egyptian vehicles and, not bothering to repaint them, drove south. In the event, 9th Brigade had already become unstuck. After a fierce battle that lasted throughout the night of 4/5 November, the

Egyptian garrison guarding the straits was forced to surrender. The two Israeli battalions that had taken the same road on the previous day arrived too late, and were already on their way back when some of the paratroopers encountered Dayan and his party. According to one version of the story they were not recognized at first and were almost killed. Then as always, commanding from the front was not without attendant risk.

Writing in the 1960s, Shimon Peres called the Suez Campaign 'one of the most brilliant of all time' and 'unequalled since the days when Hannibal crossed the snowy Alps and Genghis Khan, the mountains of Asia'.[49] In fact it was a two-division (plus two independent brigades, Sharon's and the 9th) campaign that only lasted a few days and only encountered about half of the enemy forces (the rest being held in check by the British and the French), so the praise seems slightly exaggerated. Yet there is something in what Peres said. Owing partly to political difficulties, partly to Dayan's unique combination of ruthlessness, daring and guile, the plan was indeed highly unusual. It put every known military doctrine on its head, confusing the enemy – to the point that Nasser, being told of the landing at the Mitla, exclaimed that the Israelis were 'attacking sand'[50] – and never allowing him to recover his balance once operations had started.

Claiming not to understand the acronyms being used, in particular by the Manpower Division, Dayan himself left his subordinates wide latitude in planning the details. Rarely was a commander less interested in administration and more concerned with leading from the front whenever possible. As he was later to write,[51] what he would really have liked was for a trumpet to sound, and then he, sitting astride a white horse and brandishing a sabre, would charge the enemy at the head of his troops. Since modern circumstances did not permit such a style of command, however, he did the next best thing: flying and driving all over the theatre of operations; visiting units; encouraging and occasionally firing commanders; and giving new orders at the relatively few moments when he felt that doing so was essential. Partly for political reasons – there was always the danger that the campaign might be halted by a UN-mandated ceasefire – and partly for operational ones, he felt that speed was of the essence and had to be maintained at all cost, even at the cost of proper staff-work; and even if it meant he himself was not always able to co-ordinate with GHQ.

As Dayan himself was well aware, such a style of command invited 'misfortunes'. At the highest level these were the result of his own orders or lack of them. First came Simhoni's disobedience which, had the French and the British failed to live up to their part of the conspiracy, could have put the entire campaign in jeopardy and given Israel some really tough choices. Next, there were his own contradictory orders in front of Abu Agheila, which caused unnecessary confusion and may have contributed to the failure of 38th *ugda* to take that position as planned. Indeed it could be argued that the only part of the campaign that went according to plan was the attack on Rafah, and even that was marked by such disorder that Laskov himself all but handed control of the battle over to the brigade commanders. It is true that Dayan cannot be held responsible for every error committed by his subordinates, not the least being several cases of friendly fire. It is also true, though, that his style of command invited error; already during the exercise of 1951 some of his units had fired on one another. To make things worse, and as the incidents at El Arish and on the way to the straits show all too clearly, he personally set an example of recklessness that bordered on irresponsibility. Percolating down the ranks, his devil-may-care attitude 'set the tone', as Israelis like to say.

Perhaps the best clue to the way Dayan treated the problems of command – and, as important, wanted his subordinates to treat them – is provided by an episode in which he was *not* directly involved and which, indeed, took place not only behind his back but against his orders. As we saw, the first move in the campaign had been a landing by the para-troopers to the east of the Mitla Pass. At the same time Ariel Sharon, commanding his brigade's other two battalions, drove west across the Sinai to link up with them, an aim he achieved by the evening of 30 October. Well knowing how headstrong this particular subordinate was, Dayan had issued him with strict orders not to enter the pass. Having seen little action until that point – on the way to the Mitla they had only encountered weak resistance – the paratroopers were spoiling for a fight. Whether for this reason or because, as he himself later wrote, he was worried about the possibility of an armoured Egyptian counter-attack from the north, early in the afternoon of 31 October Sharon decided to enter nevertheless.

While Sharon himself stayed where he was, i.e. outside the pass, one of his battalions drove forward in single file without either reconnoitring the terrain or occupying the hills on both sides. They came under heavy fire, were forced to halt and had to be extricated; by the time the unnec-essary battle ended thirty-eight Israelis, almost one quarter of the IDF's entire loss during the campaign, had been killed. Laskov was later appointed to carry out an investigation. He took the testimony of all involved and discovered that the chief of staff, Southern Front, Colonel Rehavan Zeevi, had in fact permitted Sharon to 'reconnoitre' the pass. Dayan himself was angry at Sharon, claiming that the latter should have levelled with him instead of resorting to a ruse – a strange demand, given that Sharon had done to Dayan no more than what both of them repeat-edly did to Lavon and Sharet. Moreover, this was not the first time Sharon, whom Dayan described as 'a gifted commander with supreme self con-fidence', had 'not known when to stop'.[52] To this extent the chief of staff only had himself to blame.

In the end, unsure of what to do, Dayan brought the matter before Ben Gurion in the latter's capacity as Minister of Defence. Ben Gurion, however, was no military man; feeling he was in no position to judge between two commanders, he let the matter drop. Privately, Dayan wrote that it was better for a commander-in-chief to 'rein in the noble steeds' than to have to 'prod the reluctant oxen'. Some years later he had the diary published, thus making his thoughts clear to the entire world. Sharon's fellow-officers were not as forgiving, accusing him of remaining outside the pass while they themselves were caught inside. As a result his career was stuck for several years, and it was only after Rabin became chief of staff in 1964 that it got under way again.

A campaign must be judged by its outcome. Dayan's belief that Arab soldiers were less than mediocre had been shaped by the early stages in his career. He saw them as immobile, systematic, and inclined towards stereo-typic action. Above all, they were incapable of taking rapid action without first waiting for orders, all of which led him to conclude that the Egyptian array in the Sinai could be 'collapsed' by guile, surprise, rapid movement and sheer bluff. However, not all his colleagues shared that feeling. At this time Laskov was commander of the armoured corps, soon to become Israel's main striking force; General Zorea, Laskov's successor, was chief of the General Staff Division of the General Staff, and General Rabin, previously head of the Training Division and, as such, responsible for IDF doctrine, was now serving as Commanding Officer, Northern Front. For weeks on end they, together with Dayan, argued over how the battle ahead should be conducted. The final part of the debate took place in the presence of Ben Gurion himself, thus offering the best possible proof that it was no mere formality. Putting the future of Israel as well as his own career on the line, Dayan promoted his ideas. But for the fact that the armoured forces played a much greater role in 'collapsing' the Egyptian Army than he had anticipated, his beliefs were vindicated. In terms of Israeli casualties suffered to Arab divisions defeated – a crude but per-haps not inaccurate measure of military excellence – the Suez Campaign was much the most successful of all Israel's wars; more successful even than the June 1967 Six Day War and certainly more successful than anything that came after that.

For Dayan personally the end of the campaign came as something of a let-down. While it would be too much to say he wanted war as such, he certainly enjoyed it for as long as it lasted. On 6 November he met Ben Gurion and told him the campaign was over: 'And you regret that, don't you?' was the response. Unlike Ben Gurion, who at one point got carried away and harangued Parliament about establishing 'the Third Kingdom of Israel', he had no patience for Messianic feelings but evaluated the campaign strictly in practical, strategic terms. For some time he hoped that Israel might retain at least the Gaza Strip and the Straits of Tyran. When American and Soviet pressure compelled Ben Gurion to return both of these to Egypt he was sorely disappointed. Though making no secret of his feelings in front of the officers of the General Staff, he steered clear of bringing the problem out into the open and turned down an offer by the editor of Israel's most important newspaper to help him do so. In the end, however hard the task, he carried out his orders strictly as he received them; there could be no question of trifling with Ben Gurion as he had with Sharet. The reopening of the straits to Israeli shipping, the right to remilitarize a small area in the western Negev and the stationing of a small force of UN observers in the Sinai were all that Israel gained from the campaign – plus, and perhaps most important of all, a well-deserved reputation for military ferocity that Dayan himself thought was essential, as well as the enhanced deterrent power that it brought in its wake.

Had it been up to him, he would have resigned almost immediately. Perhaps in order to show who was boss Ben Gurion prevented him from doing so. As always after a war, there were lessons to be learnt and reorganizations to be carried out. Dayan chaired some of the relevant

ABOVE Moshe Dayan (*first on left*) with Degania children, *c.* 1919.
© Zionist Archive, Jerusalem

BELOW Nahalal in 1933. © Israel Government Press Office

ABOVE Orde Wingate as Major General. © Corbis

OPPOSITE TOP The 1948 War: Arab Officer inspecting his men. © Corbis

RIGHT Playing in the snow, Jerusalem, winter 1950. © Zionist Archive, Jerusalem

ABOVE The 1956 War: Israeli troops in the Sinai.
© Hulton-Deutsch Collection/Corbis

1967: The Savior: 'The world asks – the Israeli people answer!', drawn by Dosh.
© Michael Gardosh. Published by kind permission of the Gardosh family.

ABOVE Moshe Dayan receiving the *Legion d'Honneur*, 1957. © Bettmann/Corbis

ABOVE On the Golan Heights, October 1973. © Bettmann/Corbis

BELOW The 1973 War: Israeli Artillery in Action. © Israel Government Press Office

TOP With Rahel, talking to a Red Cross Representative. © David Rubinger/Corbis

ABOVE With some of the Antiques found in the Gaza Strip, 1978.
© David Rubinger/Corbis

ABOVE With Prime Minister Menahem Begin. © Israel Government Press Office

BELOW The peacemaker: flying to Egypt with Ezer Weizman.
© David Rubinger/Corbis

committees, and the measures discussed in 1957 proved to be the first steps in transforming the IDF into the formidable fighting machine that revealed itself to an astounded world ten years later. Among other things he recognized his error with respect to the value of armour. The battle of Rafah, and even more the pursuit that followed, made a profound impression on him. Once the Israeli tanks had broken through the fortifications the Egyptian troops broke and ran, enabling 27th Armoured Brigade to cover 200 kilometres in five days. Now Dayan initiated the reconstruction of the IDF's ground arms around the armoured corps. He fully grasped the importance of having organic armoured brigades, although when others suggested setting up permanent armoured *divisions* he rejected the idea as being beyond the IDF's means. In the event, that step was only taken after the 1967 War. He wanted to double the size of the air force and improve the training of reserve units. He was also well aware that the navy, with its few Second World War vintage destroyers and torpedo boats, was out of date, and he initiated a re-examination of its future.

Perhaps most important, he changed the manpower system in such a way as to make sure that the IDF's officer corps would remain young. Uprisings tend to promote youth, and Israel's struggle against the British was no exception. He himself had reached the top at the age of 39. He felt that others should do the same. The way he saw it, youthful ardour was a precondition for the speed and determination that he thought would be decisive in any future war. At that time many commanders were 1948 War veterans, and forcing them into retirement did not make him any friends. Yet for many years the system of 'two careers', which kept Israeli officers much younger than their opposite numbers in other armies, served the IDF well. Had he been able to see General Headquarters as it is today, he would have been surprised at the number of grey-haired, pot-bellied commanders running, or trying to run, about.

Still, compared to the excitement of war all these were trifles that he could, and did, leave to his subordinates. Dayan himself was beginning to feel that he had done it all, seen it all. Nor did being awarded the French *Legion d'Honneur* give him any real consolation; few men were less interested in decorations and the ceremonies that came with them. At his own insistence, he stepped down from his post of chief of staff on 29 January 1958. As his parting-gift before leaving office he received a letter from Ben Gurion. The Prime Minister commended him for two 'seemingly contradictory qualities ... a daring so great as to border on madness and profound tactical and strategic wisdom'.[53] At the farewell ceremony he put on a show of modesty: in response to the praise showered on him he attributed his achievements to 'our wonderful youth, the excellent commanders, my predecessor in office, and my colleagues at work'.[54] After twenty-one years in which he had worn one kind of uniform or another almost continuously, a new phase in his life was beginning. It appears as if he did not know quite what to do with it.

CHAPTER 4

From War to War

The Israel that emerged from the Suez Campaign was a very different place from the country that, after a desperate and very bloody struggle, had gained its independence only eight years before. In 1948 the population was 650,000; in 1956 it had reached 1,600,000, and only ten years later it stood at about 2,400,000. About two-thirds of the increase consisted of new immigrants from practically every country in the world. The rest resulted from a comparatively high birthrate and, perhaps most important of all, rapidly improving standards of health, housing and social welfare. Compared with Western Europe and, *a fortiori*, the United States, Israel remained a poor country, and life for many immigrants, particularly oriental ones, was extremely hard. Nevertheless, between 1957 and 1965, when it was hit by a deep recession, Israel's economy surged to an almost 10 per cent increase per year on average. This was remarkable even for the fast growing 1960s, and greater than that of any country other than Japan. No wonder the nation felt flushed with confidence and proud of its achievements.

Some time before leaving his post Dayan, no doubt hoping to be offered some high political or administrative post, had told Ben Gurion that he wanted to study. In the Prime Minister, though, he met his master. Ben Gurion had the memory of an elephant. Perhaps he recalled an occasion in 1949 when a reporter for *Life* magazine suggested that the commander of Jerusalem might some day become Prime Minister. Perhaps he resented the way Dayan had first nudged him into launching the Sinai Campaign and then resisted the evacuation of the peninsula; or perhaps he simply wanted to give the young hothead time to cool down. Now he asked which fields interested the retiring chief of staff most. Dayan answered they were political science and oriental studies (to his daughter, he himself had condemned the former as 'a waste of time and money').[55] Yet Ben Gurion pretended to believe him. He gave it as his opinion that these were indeed very important subjects, and wished him good luck.

There was nothing for it but to carry out his threat and register at the Hebrew University in Jerusalem. In his memoirs Dayan dismisses these two years by saying that 'they were like a vacation, and like most vacations they did not leave a deep impression'.[56] This contempt for academia was a by-product of the fighting spirit he himself had done so much to instil, and was quite typical of the IDF at that time. In 1957, when Ben Gurion suggested that every officer should attend a university as a matter of right, Dayan rejected the idea. It was a suggestion to be realized only in 1997, sixteen years after his death; until then, the IDF continued to share his own belief that the best way to study war was to prepare for it and fight in it. He spent much of his time at the university cafeteria, holding court on the special floor supposedly reserved for faculty members and thus demonstrating not only his contempt for them but also his own special status. One professor, the late David Flusser, considered him the most intelligent of all the officers he taught. During examinations he cheated 'like mad', not at all abashed and not at all hindered by having just one eye. To explain why he only came home once a week he told Ruth that he was studying very hard, trying to complete a three-year course in two. He already had one year's worth of credit from Tel Aviv

University in the early 1950s. He did not, however, bother to take his degree.

He had long been a member of the ruling MAPAI Party – at that time this was not against the law, Israel being a socialist country strongly influenced by the Soviet model – and he even participated in some of its meetings. Now his attempts to enter party politics in his own right fell completely flat. He gave a few speeches about the need for people to live more frugally, to work harder, and to push the economy along so that Israel might draw level with more developed countries. His speeches were neither well considered nor supported by adequate evidence. Nor were they at all original. In fact this kind of exhortation, combined with much grumbling against 'waste', 'inefficiency', and 'favouritism', was standard fare for members of MAPAI's 'Young Guard'. The only difference was that it originated not in some unknown hothead but in the greatest warrior in the two-thousand-year history of the Jewish people.

As might be expected, he drew the applause of the young students who came to listen to him. As might also be expected, however, and as had already happened at Basel in 1946, the veteran politicians in the audience could only shake their heads at the ex-chief of staff's naïvete and total lack of understanding for socio-political realities. They demanded that Ben Gurion disown him, and even that he be prohibited from speaking in public. Meanwhile the press had a field day, caricaturing him as a naughty boy throwing stones at Party Headquarters. His only saving grace was the sense of humour that had always made up such a large part of his charm. As one story has it, a party comrade, the venerable Ms Baba Idelson, asked him why he was in such a hurry to get ahead, given that she and the other members of her generation were soon going to die anyhow. 'Because you people cannot be trusted', he shot back.

It was only after the elections of November 1959, which gave MAPAI the greatest electoral victory in Israeli history, that he became a Member of Parliament. With his experience in diplomacy he would have liked to become Minister for Foreign Affairs; since that post was being held by Ms Meir, her subsequent dislike for him is understandable. Instead Ben Gurion made him Minister of Agriculture. The post was a fairly junior one although, since establishing rural settlements in unpopulated areas was considered vital for the country's security, not as junior as it would be in other countries or, at a later time, in Israel itself. After the excitement of leading troops in battle, having to come into the office each day and engage in paperwork was a disappointment. Amidst endless petty manoeuvring between farmers, the Labour Federation, the Ministry of the Treasury, and the civil service, he was supposed to give his attention to such mundane matters as the distribution of water and the price of cows.

In the English version of his memoirs he passes very lightly over this period. In the Hebrew one he tries to put as good a face as possible on it, citing his ministry's attempts to establish new settlements, help Arab farmers, and, with US financing, assist developing countries in Asia and Africa. Not a word is wasted on his most notable 'achievement' and the one for which his term of office is remembered to this day: namely his attempt to compel farmers to grow a new brand of tomato known as 'Moneymaker' and intended for export. Though the new brand had a different shape and consistency from the old one, nothing was done to make the necessary adjustments in harvesting, packaging, transportation and marketing methods. As a result of what can only be called gross mismanagement, the effort never got off the ground; in the end, very few tomatoes were exported. To make things worse, Israeli housewives remained stubbornly loyal to the old brand, causing its price to skyrocket. In a country where no meal is complete without tomatoes, and where they are known as 'red gold', this was a minor disaster; called to account in Parliament, he answered that he was prepared to defend his tomatoes to the last drop of juice in the opposition's veins. Tomatoes, however, were no joking matter. He emerged from the episode with the epithet 'General Moneymaker' attached to his name.

As a minister, he continued his old and trusted methods of focusing on perhaps four to five selected fields that interested him most, and treating the rest as if they did not exist. He also spent much time out of the office, giving his subordinates wide latitude. As a one-on-one negotiator he excelled, leaving no stone unturned in his efforts to reach an agreement, but as a committee man charged with gathering votes he felt lost. As a member of the cabinet he was difficult to deal with and, some would say, disloyal to his colleagues; for most of them he felt nothing but contempt. In part, this was because they were elderly and civilian. Many of them represented just the kind of 'Diaspora Jew' that Zionism had set out to eradicate. This was true to the point that, among themselves, they still talked in Yiddish; and it was precisely those people who were holding back native-born, young, dynamic fighters such as he.

Much of his time was spent quarrelling with the Minister of the Treasury – he happened to be Levy Eshkol – and with the Minister of Trade and Industry, Pinhas Sapir, over budgets, priorities, allocations, prices and everything else. Sapir, a human bulldozer who was soon to become one of the most powerful figures in Israeli politics, resented Dayan's domineering ways and poked fun at 'the Field Marshal who pretends to know about subsidies for eggs'. Eshkol, who was as well-balanced and affable as Dayan was mercurial and abrasive, nicknamed him 'Abu Gilda' after a well-known Arab terrorist leader of the 1930s. In fact he never shook off his image as a naughty *moshav* boy. To a large extent, it was his own fault. Even while he was serving as chief of staff he would invite his fellow officers to go stealing oranges with him. Told that they might be caught in the act, he answered, with childish pride, that 'I don't get caught'. Once, in fact, he *was* caught; however, seeing that he was no 'ordinary thief', instead of landing a cudgel on his head the watchman let him go. On another occasion he escaped being ticketed for fast driving by telling the policeman that, since he only had one eye, he could only see half of the speedometer.

In June 1963 Ben Gurion, now an old man living in the past and interested in nothing so much as settling scores that nobody else could remember, resigned. In both his posts – Prime Minister and Minister of Defence – he was succeeded by Levy Eshkol. The new Prime Minister had no need of Dayan's advice; for that he relied on Rabin, whom he himself had appointed chief of staff and whom he treated like an oracle. Deprived of Ben Gurion's support, Dayan soon found that he was no match for the new Prime Minister and the senior members of MAPAI; much more experienced than he, they checkmated him at every move. For another unhappy year he held on to his post. He quarrelled with everybody and would wake up in the morning to find that plans for settling entire districts had been made and approved behind his back.

In November 1964 he handed in his resignation – 'as long as I am still able to stand on my feet',[57] as he put it. Seven months later Ben Gurion called on him to show his loyalty by joining his own newly formed opposition party, RAFI. Dayan well knew that, in a country dominated by MAPAI, doing so was political suicide and events proved him right. Nevertheless, he did not think he had a choice and, together with Shimon Peres, found himself on Ben Gurion's side. His time as minister had taught him that he was not cut out for the rough and tumble of party politics and the petty haggling it involves. He also concluded he would never become Prime Minister.[58] As he saw it, occupying that office would only oblige him to deal with a host of matters he considered of secondary importance, be it making speeches, lunching with foreign heads of state, canvassing for votes, or anything else.

Upon leaving office he asked Eshkol for, and received – like a bone thrown to a dog – a directorship of a public fishing company which soon failed. As a member of the opposition he was hopeless. He left the day-to-day work of canvassing, organizing, fund-raising, etc., to Peres, who was as good at it as Dayan was bad. What is more, he retained his independence. At least twice he sided with MAPAI against RAFI. The first time was when Ben Gurion accused Eshkol, for whom he now bore an intense hatred, of neglecting Israel's security. He was referring to the development of nuclear weapons which, according to foreign sources, was going on at Dimona in the Negev. Along with Peres, Dayan had supported the project in its early stages and was well aware of what was going on in Dimona; he felt there was nothing wrong with what Eshkol was doing and did not hesitate to say so openly. The second time was in November 1966 when he refused to condemn Eshkol for launching a retaliatory strike (in which some thirty Jordanian soldiers were killed) in response to an attack on an Israeli bus. As somebody said, he was not so much a party man as a one-man party. On the few occasions when he presented himself in Parliament he would sit at his own table in the House restaurant. There, few people dared join him uninvited.

His failure to make his mark as a politician did not affect his fame, which kept growing. Already during the late 1950s his house in Nahalal had become an object of pilgrimage for visitors from all over the world. They came to see, hear and smell the place that had given birth to their great hero; the fact that he no longer lived there at any time after his period as Commanding Officer, Northern Front, did not seem to bother them. He understood the importance of the media and got along very well with them. In part it was his sharp tongue and capacity for prompt repartee, in part his sense of humour which, to his credit, he always directed at his superiors rather than at those who worked for him. Perhaps most important was his unique ability to disguise his deviousness with a show of honesty. Later, when he had to represent Israel to the world, this was to serve him well.

In spite of everything, he was bored; being bored, he had much time left for his hobby, archaeology. He had always been a sensuous man and enjoyed doing things with his hands, whether ploughing a field, helping a cow deliver its calf, or constructing furniture. Digging up old artefacts, however, was something else. It appealed both to the link he felt to the Bible and to his highly developed aesthetic sensibility; the fact that there was something illicit about it may have increased its attraction in his eyes. As chief of staff, and later even as Minister of Defence, he misused his authority to declare newly discovered sites off limits to archaeologists. Next, having taken what he wanted, he would order army vehicles to carry the finds, some of which were man-sized and very heavy, to his home. Even in the Israel of that time, a country that, because of its socialist traditions, did not draw as strict a line between the private and the public as supposedly exists in other democratic states, his behaviour raised eyebrows. In the end, though, his 'hard-won merits' – as the saying went – and sheer impudence always carried him through. When there was talk of prosecuting him he dared people to do their worst, saying he would neither deny responsibility nor hide behind his parliamentary immunity. If he was never put on trial then this says as much about the society as about him. At that time even more than today, circumstances compelled Israel to live by sacrificing its sons' blood; hence it was prepared to overlook their indiscretions.

Many of the stolen artefacts were broken and had to be reconstructed. It was work that required great patience and at which he developed much skill. Wearing khaki clothes and an old hat, he would spend hours sitting cross-legged on the ground while handling various acids, files, glues, and the like; once, asked what he was doing, he said that what he was really digging up were his own thoughts. Over the years there rose a magnificent collection, some of it found in the field and the rest purchased from dealers, which occupied most of his garden. He rigged up an illumination system in order to display it at night; not only did he show it to visitors, but he used it as a prop to relieve the tension during negotiations. The pieces he wanted he selected according to aesthetic criteria rather than with a view to any scientific value. Many were encrusted in a patina of dirt. He developed a sort of sixth sense which enabled him to guess which ones were the most beautiful underneath; colleagues who left him free to choose newly discovered artefacts, sight unseen, often rued the day. Those he did not want he sold, again illegally, but not before marking them with a certificate saying they originated in 'the private collection of Moshe Dayan'.

Perhaps because he had grown up in poverty, perhaps because of the humiliation involved in having to ask favours from his rich parents-in-law (he only became completely independent of them in 1963), he was developing an interest in money. Already in the mid 1960s he felt delighted if his daughter, then a young writer making her way in the world, paid his expenses when he visited her abroad; later the interest grew into a passion. His fame, which among other things enabled him to buy the objects he wanted with cheques he knew would not be cashed, helped. So did his hobby; not long after his death, the Israel Museum paid one million US dollars for his collection. Before it was broken up and the individual pieces sent to the departments where they belonged, it was put on display one last time, attracting large crowds. Nor was this the end of the story. To make his garden accommodate his finds, Dayan had commandeered part of the pavement in front of his house. After his death the wall was pulled down, by Arab labourers no less. *Sic transit gloria mundi.*

The other 'interest' that brought him to life was, of course, women. His home life had long fallen apart. In spite of some difficulties – his absences caused Ruth to complain that he neglected her, and she cried a lot – the Dayan marriage seems to have been happy at first. In 1944–45, when the role he played in the 'Season' compelled him to move from Nahalal to Tel Aviv, he insisted that Ruth and the children follow him there. The way he saw it, a family was hard enough to keep together even without physical separation; later Yael was to write that her parents made love almost every night. Perhaps the example he had in mind was that of his father. Whether through his own fault or through Dvora's, during his travels Shmuel had become estranged from his wife. He had a string of mistresses and ended up living with one of them in Jerusalem; meanwhile Dvora, depressed but immensely stubborn, vegetated in Nahalal. As late as 1950, when the battalion commanders' course often took him to Israel's northern border, Moshe insisted on going home to Jerusalem each night. The distance was well over a hundred miles. He always drove very fast – had he been ticketed, as ordinary mortals are, he would have gone bankrupt – and made his driver do the same. Still, such was the state of Israeli roads at the time that the journey must have taken at least three hours.

In 1953 the family moved to Zahala – from ZAHAL, the Hebrew acronym for the IDF – a new suburb perhaps 8 miles north-east of Tel Aviv which was being built especially for senior officers like him. Here they occupied a three-bedroom house with their two sons, Ehud (Udi) and Asaf (Asi). Yael, an early developer, was already giving the first signs of wanting to leave home. Not long after, the man who had once lectured a girl about the importance of sexual purity turned into an insatiable womanizer, changing mistresses as other men do socks. At least one was among his daughter's best friends; but there were also a few with the artistic sensitivity to describe what it was like. Much later, a doctor allegedly told Yael that the problem, if a problem it was, had its origin in his injury which had created scar tissue which pressed on the brain. Whether she believed him or not is unclear.

Something of his attitude to women comes through from the following episode. The early 1950s were a period of very great financial difficulty for the IDF. During the first half of 1953, in his capacity as chief of the General Staff Branch, Dayan was doing whatever he could to increase the fighting 'teeth' at the expense of the service 'tail'. As well as changing his own car and office for more modest ones, he proposed to replace senior commanders' cars with jeeps. In this way those commanders' wives, worried about what the wind might do to their hairdos and dust to their dresses, would stop using the vehicles for their private ends; he himself, incidentally, continued to drive a jeep until his election to Parliament. Jeeps being more expensive to run than ordinary cars, the proposal was rejected. Still it is illuminating. As at least one of his mistresses wrote,[59] at bottom he was contemptuous of women. Whether the contempt was 'inborn' or resulted from some specific experience is not clear; certainly he would not be the first man who turned to many women after having suffered disappointment at the hands of the one he really loved. Be this as it may, the less attention he paid them the more they ran after him, often taking the initiative, seeking him out and throwing themselves at him – each one, of course, hoping she might be the one to make him love her and her alone.

Making full use of his fame – given his distinct appearance, he could not have avoided doing so even if he had wanted – his method of approaching a female target was direct, almost brutal. He might start by saying 'come and dance, beautiful woman!' If she responded, he would use some pointed metaphor to make his desire clear; perhaps because he did not try to hide anything, words that would have been offensive if used by others did not sound so when coming from his mouth. Later, he would turn some apt phrase to make a woman feel that she was special and that, for the moment at any rate, she alone could relieve his apparent weariness. Along with this he brought a good sense of humour and, most important of all, his usual ability to poke fun at himself. For example, he was capable of turning the common cliché on its head and pretend to lament the 'fact' that a woman was only interested in his body.

That body was on the heavy side and very powerful. When he wanted to he could be a real 'sexpert', alternately passionate, skilful and considerate. At his best he enjoyed a woman's enjoyment as much as the act itself and seemed astonished by the pleasure he gave her; once it was over, he often found some nice way to compliment her on the pleasure she gave him. If a woman met his approval he would read her some of the Hebrew poetry he loved and in which he found the 'simplicity, noble, pure, aesthetic'[60] he longed for. If she was active outside her home, she might arrive at work to find the unexpected apple, or bar of chocolate, left by him with a short poem praising, say, her beautiful hair. However, there is no record of him making expensive presents or taking a woman on vacation with him. Everybody knew he was married, nor did he make a secret of the fact that the arrangement suited him and he wished to remain so; if he could be arrogant, at least he did not lie or pretend to have tender feelings that were not there. The quality that made him hardest to deal with was his elusiveness. A woman would see him only as often, and for as long, as he wanted.

Most of his women were one-night stands. Some lasted longer, and a few of those he even introduced to his daughter in an attempt to gain her approval. Among other things, it was his way of showing her how much he appreciated her; needless to say, it did not work. Among those who lasted longest was one Hadasa Mor. Thin, good-looking and twenty years younger than him, they first met in 1955. At that time she had just become the lover of an officer who happened to be an acquaintance of Dayan from his Hagana days, a Lieutenant-Colonel Dov Yirmiya. Yirmiya, who was married, asked Dayan for help in divorcing his wife. Dayan did, in fact, talk to the wife, but apparently was so interested in what Yirmiya had said about his pert-nosed mistress that he invited both of them to

dinner at his house, a great honour. She was young, but not innocent.
By her own account, no sooner did she set eyes on him than she decided
that, no matter how, one day she would sleep with this 'real man'.

In the event Yirmiya did divorce his wife and did marry Ms Mor. Some
time after this, Dayan came to visit her and the newlywed found herself
in his arms – 'like a lamb in the maw of a wolf that had trapped her by
deceit'.[61] The affair started during the period he was studying in Jerusalem
– he had an apartment there, and only returned to Zahala on the weekends – and she took an apartment next to his; at the time it ended he
was Minister of Agriculture and lived in the town's most expensive hotel.
Seeing that he insisted on calling the shots and also had trysts with other
women, repeatedly she broke it off; only to resume it when he, half-
irritated by her antics and half amused by them, demanded that she yield.
In the meantime, perhaps in order to excite his jealousy, she also had an
affair with another man. After he finally sent her away for good she
described her experiences in a thinly disguised autobiographical novel.
Before she published it she tried to blackmail him and was told to go to
hell. Once she did publish it became the talk of the town, causing his
family much pain. He himself dismissed it as trash, and rightly so. It is
so banal ('looking naughtily across my shoulder, I approached him with
cat-like steps') that one can read all 265 pages without being any the
wiser about what made him or, for that matter her, tick. Apparently her
favourite activity was putting her bathrobe on and off.

The tangle had a curious appendix. In his anguish Yirmiya turned to
Prime Minister Ben Gurion, asking him to call the 'one-eyed one', as he
called him, to account. Not long after, afraid she was about to lose her
husband to Ms Mor, Ruth Dayan did the same. Ben Gurion's own wife
was the formidable Paula. During his younger days he had not been
unknown to stray from her, whereupon she took to watching him like a
she-dragon. Perhaps this helps explain his response. He told them both

in no uncertain terms that Moshe's behaviour in his private life was none of his concern; nor would he consider it when the time came to decide on the future of this exceptionally talented soldier who had served his country so well. To Yirmiya he added that Hadasa was, after all, as much to blame as was Moshe. Much later, as a leading member of the feminist lobby in Israel's Parliament, Yael promoted the idea that women are too feeble-minded to say 'No' to a man who wants them. In 1957, though, that notion had not yet entered anybody's head; to her credit, Ms Mor never pretended otherwise. If she is to be believed Yirmiya took the episode very badly, raving, comparing himself with Uria (whose wife, Bath Sheba, had been seduced by King David), and even battering her. Ruth's reaction is not recorded. She always was, and according to her grandson remains (at the age of 83) an active, warm, well-balanced and brave woman. As far as is known, it was the only time she ever asked for help. Early in 2001 she wrote the introduction to a new collection of the letters he had sent her from prison; if she was bitter, then she did not complain. Moshe knew all this and respected her. Had it depended on him, he would never have been divorced.

Dayan shared Ben Gurion's belief that a person's private life had nothing to do with his public functions. This was a period when, in Israel and perhaps in other democratic countries as well, people still expected to look up to and respect politicians; the best thing one could say about anybody was that he or she set a 'shining example'. Dayan was exceptional in that he refused to shine. The way he saw it, his life was his own. His official duties apart, what he did with it was entirely his business. It was his good fortune that, at that time even less than now, Israeli society was not as puritanical or as hypocritical as some others. His well-known philandering did not affect either his career or his popularity, and the latter may even have benefited from it. Part of his notoriety was due to envy. He realized this, and it probably made him even more

contemptuous of humanity than he already was; as he once said, what
many other men did in secret he did publicly and without trying to conceal his tracks. Still, on occasion even he must have found the endless
gossip and coarse joking hard to bear. In one conversation with Peres –
during the period when both were in the opposition they lunched
together every week – he asked what people wanted from him; after all,
'have I ever drowned a girl in a river?'[62]

By that time Ruth and he were leading largely separate lives. Beginning
around 1952–53 she developed into a public personality in her own right.
Relying on immigrant labour, she founded and ran a network of work-
shops and dealerships that specialized in oriental clothes, jewelry, rugs
and the like. Soon the house in Zahala became as cluttered with them as
the garden was by archaeological finds. Somewhat to her own surprise
she also turned into an effective public speaker and fund-raiser, travelling
all over the Western world. Her appeal to Ben Gurion apart, she was too
proud to complain about her domestic trouble. Dayan on his part was
too proud to lie to her or hold her against her will. In spite of everything
they still had their good moments together, which may be one reason
why she stayed with him for as long as she did. In the end, unable to
stand the humiliation any longer, it was she who asked for a divorce.

Of Dayan's three children, Yael had always been his favourite. Judging
by what she wrote of their relationship, to some extent she seems to have
taken Ruth's place; though she was not uncritical of him, they remained
on good terms until he died. By contrast, his sons ceased to interest him
once they had reached puberty. They in turn spent much of their youth
trying to get away from the Dayan legend and be their own persons. Not,
however, with success; these were the years when, during the Israeli equivalent of Hallowe'en, every second child would put on a black patch and
pretend he was the hero. Later they turned against him with great
bitterness, accusing him of neglect, meanness and much else. This was

particularly true of the youngest, Asaf. He had a highly original mind that he used to make excellent films; in between he drifted in and out of mental institutions. Since Moshe had never made any bones of the fact that he did not want children, to some extent the problem must have been rooted in his relations with Ruth, yet in no recorded utterance did he ever level accusations at her. In his letters to her, he always assumed the full blame for whatever difficulties he and she had.

Normally he was cool and detached, but from time to time there would be displays of affection to those who surrounded him. Jonathan Gefen, the son of Moshe's sister Aviva who, as a teenager during the early 1960s, spent time living in the Dayan household, described what it was like. Out of the blue came a kiss on the head, a request to read a poem (Gefen was to become one of Israel's best-known writers, and was already exercising his poetic muscle) and a well-crafted compliment. At night, both of them suffered from the family disease of insomnia. Often he would hear his uncle's heavy tread as he went to the kitchen; next Moshe would enter his nephew's room to offer a piece of chocolate. The method, if a method it was, worked as well within the family as it did with strangers. As Gefen wrote, 'it was easy to admire Moshe'.[63]

In 1965, he brought out *Sinai Diary*; with its non-technical, restrained yet occasionally poetical language, the book proved he could not merely fight but write as well. The next year he received an offer from *Maariv*, at that time Israel's largest newspaper, to go to Vietnam and report on the war there; the articles that resulted were also published in the British and French press. Dayan knew nothing about Vietnam and prepared himself thoroughly, travelling by way of France, Britain and the United States to meet some experts and talk over the war with them. In Paris he met several generals who had commanded in Indo-China and whom, having co-operated with them at the time of the 1956 Campaign, he felt he could trust. One of them told him that the enemy was elusive and that the voyage was a waste of time since he would see nothing; typically, his response was that at least he would see that he could not see and that doing so would be instructive in itself.[64] In Britain he met Field Marshal Montgomery who told him to tell the Americans, in his name, that they were insane. He also said that Wingate, whom Dayan admired so much, had been mentally unbalanced and that the best thing he ever did was to get himself killed in a plane crash in 1944. In spite of the old man's bluntness, their conversation was friendly enough. At no point did Dayan feel Montgomery was out to offend him personally.

In Washington, DC he talked to various officers as well as officials of the State Department and the National Security Council. At the Pentagon he was impressed by the arrogance – unspoken and sometimes spoken – that stemmed from American power and technological prowess. There and elsewhere the dominant feeling was that people were very committed and worked very hard; however, they did not really know where they were heading. His most important contact in Washington was the Secretary of Defence, Robert McNamara. Contrary to his reputation, McNamara was pleasant and approachable and did what he could to answer all of the questions addressed to him by Dayan and some of the others present. He did not, however, succeed in convincing Dayan either that the American presence in Vietnam was inherently different from that of their French predecessors or that they stood a better chance of winning the war. Perhaps one reason for this was because, as we now know, he was already having his own doubts; which indeed led to his resignation in the next year. On the flight from Honolulu to Tokyo Dayan summed up his impressions. He knew the Europeans could not compete with the US, militarily speaking, and so of course did the Europeans themselves. Nevertheless, the way he saw it, the Americans, by ignoring European attitudes to the war, were making a *big* mistake.

Arriving in Vietnam on 25 July, his first stop was Saigon where there was paperwork to be done and where, like most visitors, he was much impressed by the incomparable beauty of the Vietnamese women in their *ao-dais*. In between he met a Vietnamese professor of nuclear physics; the latter told him – in strict confidence, since saying anything contrary to the official line was dangerous – that the Vietcong were much stronger than the Americans knew or wanted to know. He also met the South Vietnamese Deputy Prime Minister and Minister of Defence, General Nguyen Van Thieu, as well the chief of the General Staff of the Army of the Republic of Vietnam. Both, he thought, were highly intelligent men. Both, interestingly enough, reserved their greatest admiration not for some American commander but for the North-Vietnamese General Giap. Giap had been the hero of the Viet Minh's struggle against the French. Now, Dayan's interlocutors hoped, he might force Hanoi to make peace.

A few days after arriving he was taken aboard the largest aircraft carrier then cruising off the Vietnamese coast, *Constellation*. Needless to say he had often read and heard about such ships, yet the vessel made a 'breathtaking' impression on him. Protected 'from the air, the sea, the ground, outer space, and under water', in reality it was a vast floating factory whose product was firepower. Every 90 minutes, amidst a numbing outburst of fire and noise, flights of combat aircraft took off to strike at targets in Vietnam. When it came to specifying the precise nature of those targets, though, his hosts refused to answer his questions; one might think they were attacking Afghanistan in 2001–2002. He ended the day by noting that 'the Americans are not fighting against infiltration to south [Vietnam], or against guerrillas, or against North Vietnamese leader Ho Chi Minh, but against the entire world. Their real aim was to show everybody – including Britain, France and the Soviet Union – their power and determination in order to pass this message: wherever Americans go, they are irresistible'.[65]

The next month or so was spent visiting various units throughout South Vietnam. First he went to see the Marines, joining a company that was patrolling only about a mile south of the Demilitarized Zone in order to prevent infiltration from the north. The company commander was a first lieutenant by the name of Charles Krulak. For three days they trudged up and down hills, wading through streams and sometimes almost drowning in them; thirty-five years later General (ret.) Krulak, ex-commandant of the Marine Corps, told me that Dayan had asked them what they were doing there. He gave it as his opinion that the American strategy was wrong, and that they should be 'where the people are' rather then chasing the Vietcong in the mountains.[66]

A few days later, at Danang, he saw other Marine units engaging in pacification. He left the district clear in his own mind that much remained to be done, so much so that it was doubtful whether the Americans were making any progress at all in trying to win hearts and minds. Nor was he impressed with the attempts to help the South Vietnamese peasants improve their standard of living by introducing new methods, better livestock and so on. This was a field where he had some experience both as a farmer and as Minister of Agriculture when, with US financial backing, he had sent experts to carry out agrarian reforms in various Asian and African countries. He had visited some of those countries in person, only to find out how hard it was to make an established culture change its ways; doing so in the midst of a war, when every achievement was under constant threat, was much harder still.

Another extremely interesting visit was the one he paid to 1st Air Cavalry Division. Organized only a few years previously, it was the most up-to-date fighting force in the world. Incredible economic, industrial and logistic power had been employed to make such a unit possible in the first place, not to mention supporting it in battle thousands of miles away from the American homeland. Operating under conditions of absolute air superiority – in all South Vietnam, there was not a single enemy aircraft – the division was capable of doing as it pleased, requiring no more than four hours' warning to land an entire battalion at any location within its helicopters' range. As it turned out, though, often four hours were four hours too many. Arriving at the selected spot, the troops would find that the enemy had gone.

It must have been during his stay with 1st Cavalry that the following incident took place. As was his custom Dayan wanted to visit the front which, in the case of Vietnam, meant going on patrol. His hosts reluctantly agreed, but fearing lest something might happen to the celebrity for whom they were responsible, selected a route that was supposedly free of the Vietcong. As often happened, their information proved wrong. They came under fire and were 'pinned down', as the phrase went. Looking around from where he was lying, the American captain in charge discovered that Dayan had disappeared. In the end he located him; the 51-year-old visitor from Israel was sitting comfortably on top of a grassy knoll. With great effort, the captain crawled to him and asked what he was doing. 'What are *you* doing?' was his answer: 'Get your ... up here, and see what this battle is all about'.

The way Dayan saw it, the problem was intelligence.

> According to Norton's (commanding officer, 1st Air Cavalry) information, there was a Vietcong division in this highland area. It was not concentrated in a single base but split into several battalions, each of about 350 men. It was Norton's plan to land a battalion ... in the Vietcong divisional area and then, in accordance with the developments of the battle, to rush in additional 'reaction troops' to reinforce, seal off and carry out flank attacks. All this was fine, except for one small item missing in the plan: the exact location of the Vietcong

battalions was not known. Air photos and air reconnaissance had failed to pick out their encampments, entrenched, bunkered and camouflaged with the jungle vegetation. The US intelligence sources were largely technical – air photos and decoded radio intercepts, for Vietcong units from battalion strength and up used transmitters. Only scanty information could be gleaned from POWs [many of whom spat in the Americans' faces and swore to die rather than talk].

The battle procedures of the 1st Cavalry operated like an assembly belt. First came the shelling of the landing zones by ground artillery. Then came aerial bombardment. And the landings themselves were covered by 'gunships', the accompanying, close-support, heli-borne, units firing their rockets and machine guns almost at our feet.

It was an amazing operation, 'but where was the war? It was like watching military manoeuvres – with only one side. [...] Where were the Vietcong? And where was the battle? The Vietcong were there, a few hundred yards away. And the battle came half an hour later when the company which had landed 300 yards to our south ran into an ambush after it had started moving off'. Within minutes the company was shot to pieces, suffering twenty-five dead and some fifty wounded including its commander. Calling in their firepower, 1st Cavalry gave pursuit. When they met resistance they would radio for the same heavy B-52 bombers which, as these words are being written, are among the aircraft deployed against Afghanistan; to what effect, was not clear.[67]

To recount each and every detail of Dayan's visit would be tedious. Everywhere he was met with the greatest courtesy and was given a more or less free hand to see and ask what he wanted. As he noted, American officers were committed, very hard working, and as frank as circumstances permitted. The commander of Military Assistance Command, Vietnam (MACV), General Westmoreland, he found pleasant and informal; however, he lacked that 'astute expression' he had discerned with a few other senior commanders. One of their great problems was the need to get their names mentioned by the media in order to advance their careers, and this did not turn them into better people or, more important, into better commanders. He admired the American rank and file, particularly the Marines and the Green Berets. They were well trained, physically fit and, in 1966, still did their job willingly. They were, to use his own Hebrew phrase, 'golden guys'; they on their part found him easy to communicate with, charming, and possessed of a sneaky sense of humour. He was even more impressed by the tremendous muscle that enabled 1,700 helicopters to be deployed in a single theatre of war. It also enabled a single operation by a single South Korean infantry company to be supported by more artillery rounds – 21,000 of them – than had been expended by all Israeli forces in the wars of 1948 and 1956 combined.

Still, nothing could make up for the lack of accurate and timely tactical intelligence. In its absence, the Americans were using sledgehammers to knock holes in empty air. Even if they did succeed, it was not easy to see how the South Vietnamese would be able to set up a viable government in the shadow of the gigantic machine that 'protected' them; whether that machine would ever be withdrawn from South East Asia was anybody's guess. As to what he was told of the war's objectives, such as defending democracy and helping the South Vietnamese people, he considered it 'childish' propaganda; if many of the Americans he met believed in them, clearly nobody else did. Over a year before the Tet Offensive showed everyone that something was very, very wrong, he left Vietnam with the definite impression that things were not going at all well. In his own words, 'the Americans are winning everything – except the war'.[68] Perhaps this was one reason why, instead of flying home by way of the United States as he had promised to do, he chose the other route. The last thing he wanted was to rub salt into the Americans' wounds, and the trip had been a welcome opportunity to keep his military knowledge up to date.

In works written about Dayan by himself and others the period between 1957 and 1967 is usually dismissed in a few pages. In fact it was extremely important to his development and to that of the country in which he lived. While serving as a cabinet minister during Israel's first years he learnt his limitations, concluding that he was not cut out to be a politician in the ordinary sense of that term. He renounced any hope of ever becoming Prime Minister. He believed his career was more or less over; had history not changed its course, he might even have resigned his seat in Parliament. The visit to Vietnam came as a relief and enabled him to draw some extremely interesting lessons from what he saw and heard. Whether he was right in his belief that the war could not be won and was, in effect, a huge mistake, is not at issue here.

Dayan's prevailing attitude in this period seems to have been one of intense boredom. Though he liked adulation and revelled in it as much as anybody, he became increasingly moody and disdainful of humanity, problems that ancient jars and a never-ending parade of more or less beautiful, more or less cultivated women could solve only partially, if at all. What makes his attitude all the more remarkable is the sharp contrast between it and that of the society in which he lived. Though still extremely small and poor, Israel was flexing its muscles and becoming one of the most dynamic countries on earth. It was also well aware of its success and immensely proud of it. Though intensely patriotic, Dayan did not share in this mood and was becoming increasingly detached. This was carried to the point where, after he had left the government, he became something of a *bête noire*; during his journey to Vietnam, the Israeli Foreign Ministry prohibited its embassies from giving him any (official) help. Though he was not depressed in the ordinary sense of the word, at least one of the women who knew him during this period actually thought that it would have been better for him if he had died a hero's death during the Suez Campaign. Then came the 1967 War, and destiny caught up with him once again.

CHAPTER 5

Saviour and Idol

While Dayan tried to allay his boredom in potsherds and women, Israel's borders remained in a fairly turbulent state. The main trouble was Syria, whose army, as the British military attaché in Damascus wrote, wanted nothing so much as to 'flatten' Israel.[69] Specifically, differences arose over Israel's project to pump water out of the Sea of Galilee in order to irrigate the Negev Desert. In January 1964 the First Arab Summit resolved to respond by diverting the sources of the Jordan away from the sea. A detailed plan for the project was drawn up and submitted to the Second Summit, which was held in September of the same year. Three months later, work started.

Then as today, Israel was basically an arid country. Then as today, about two-thirds of its entire water resources were concentrated in the Sea of Galilee. Hence it is scarcely surprising that the attempt to divert the sources of the Jordan was considered intolerable and needed to be stopped by every possible means. It was important, however, to avoid the onus of being the first to open fire, and so Eshkol, in consultation with Rabin, resorted to a stratagem. In 1949 the armistice agreements between Israel and Syria had established three small demilitarized areas totalling a few hundred acres. Israel had long argued that they consti-tuted sovereign territory – which they did – and that it had the right to work them down to the very last yard. Now, pushing forward, it began to make good its word. Seeing the tractors move, the Syrian troops on the Golan Heights would open fire both on them and on the *kibbutzim* in the Jordan valley.

Throughout 1965 the incidents escalated. First the Israelis used tank-fire to hit their opponents' earth-moving equipment. Next, when the Syrians changed the route of the canal they were digging in order to increase the range, Rabin called in the air force. The Syrians in turn sent up fighters, leading to several air-to-air combats; in the summer of 1966, their attempt to divert the water had to be given up. This, however, did not bring an end to the incidents, as Syrian Intelligence supported the newly formed Palestinian Liberation Organization (PLO) and stepped up terrorist attacks inside Israel. Along the Golan Heights, too, the two sides continued to skirmish; each time the Israelis moved a tractor into one of the disputed areas the Syrians would open artillery fire on the settlements below. The largest incident took place on 7 April 1967 when 240 shells destroyed the *kibbutz* of Gadot and no fewer than six Syrian fighters were shot down. On 11 May, Eshkol said that an Israeli action 'larger than that of 7 April' might be necessary. Three days later Rabin agreed, giving four different interviews to four different newspapers in which he said that more operations might be called for, even to the point of toppling the *Baath* regime in Damascus.[70]

Dayan, who during most of this time was a member of the opposition, was only involved in a marginal way. He and Rabin had never got along. Before the Suez Campaign, to prevent the latter from 'getting in our way',[71] he appointed him to the post of Commanding Officer, Northern Front. Rabin in turn disliked Dayan's 'partisanic' methods, calling him 'a user of force, not a builder of force'.[72] Perhaps more important than the personal likes and dislikes was a change in attitude. From about 1966 onwards the man who once wanted Israel to behave like 'a rabid dog' became less hawkish. Speaking to Peres in private, he gave it as his opinion that, in their anti-Syrian policy, Eshkol and Rabin were 'out of their minds' and would lead the country to war.[73] It is claimed that, in the last interview he gave not long before his death, he said that Israel's tactic had been to 'bug' the Syrians by driving a tractor along the border until they opened fire.[74] Yet he was careful not to say anything in public. Perhaps, having learnt his lesson in 1958–64, he feared lest speaking out would only make him even more isolated than he already was. Or perhaps he did not want to split public opinion, which swallowed its government's propaganda and seemed determined to enforce Israel's sovereignty to the last field and to the last furrow.

In the end, his return to power was occasioned by a major blunder on the part of Rabin. Counselled by his chief of intelligence, General Aharon Yariv, Rabin – with Eshkol's support – believed that, since the Egyptian Army was bogged down in Yemen, he could move against Syria with impunity. As it turned out this was far from being the case. His warnings to that country compelled Nasser, who, as the self-styled leader of the Arab world could not stand by while Syria was being threatened, to come to the latter's aid; at the same time it gave him a welcome excuse to pull out of Yemen. On 15 May powerful Egyptian forces began marching into the Sinai, taking up positions facing the Israeli border and presenting a direct threat. On 16 May the UN Force that had been stationed there since 1957 was asked to leave, and on 23 May the Straits of Tyran were once again closed to Israeli shipping. Subsequently Syria, Jordan and Iraq all jumped on the Egyptian bandwagon, mobilizing, deploying troops and entering into military alliances. From Cairo to Baghdad, Arab capitals filled with dancing, chanting crowds demanding that the Jews be slaughtered.

These events struck Israel 'like a bolt from the blue'.[75] For the first time since 1948 the country's existence appeared to be in mortal danger; as almost two hundred thousand men were called up and the economy ground to a halt, parks were being ritually consecrated to serve as cemeteries if necessary. In the midst of what almost amounted to a national panic, a search for solutions got under way. Dayan himself asked Eshkol for, and was reluctantly given, permission to visit the Israeli troops now deploying along the Egyptian border in order to study their plans and capabilities at first hand; during the next few days he talked to all three divisional commanders as well as nine brigade commanders. On 22 May Rabin came to see him, having previously visited Ben Gurion who had minced no words in blaming him [i.e. Rabin] for the 'adventurist' policy that had put Israel in danger. Unlike his former superior, Dayan was too tactful to berate the overworked chief of staff for past mistakes. Instead, he said that he [i.e. Dayan] 'was *also* [my emphasis] surprised at Nasser's willingness to fight.'

Both of them agreed that Eshkol was not providing proper leadership and that the Prime Minister did not seem able to make up his mind about how to deal with the situation. His attempts, and those of Foreign Minister Abba Eban, to enlist the 'Great Powers' to Israel's side appeared futile and even humiliating. He did not seem to have what was needed to take the country to war and had already postponed that decision several times; in a radio address to the nation he had stammered, making the worst possible impression. As to Rabin, Dayan thought he looked tired, which he considered understandable, but also confused and demoralized, which was not: 'If this is the way he addresses the troops', he wrote in his diary, 'then things are bad indeed'. Rabin in turn was glad to hear that Dayan had found the IDF in an excellent state. As he wrote, whatever his other faults he could not be blamed for having failed to prepare for war.[76]

The next few days brought many more complicated manoeuvres. There was talk of bringing Ben Gurion into the cabinet. However, Eshkol refused; having suffered years of vicious attacks, he said that 'these two horses will no longer pull together'. Dayan himself well realized that Eshkol and his cronies – above all, Golda Meir, then MAPAI Secretary General – did not want him as Minister of Defence. He played his cards well, making no moves on his own behalf and refusing various unimportant posts that the Prime Minister tried to foist on him. Instead he suggested that he take over as Commanding Officer, Southern Front. This would have put him in charge of an eventual war with Israel's most dangerous enemy; but Rabin, who did not want such an unruly subordinate, persuaded Eshkol against it. Seeing that giving up his portfolio as Minister of Defence was inevitable, Eshkol tried to give it to Allon, then serving as Deputy Prime Minister. However, Allon's military laurels had faded. Few remembered his role in 1948 when he had been Israel's most successful field commander.

Late in May, the pressure on Eshkol mounted. Some of it originated in public opinion, including Israel's leading daily newspaper and a group of prominent ladies known as 'the Merry Wives of Windsor'. Some came from Menahem Begin, the former ETZEL leader. For many years Begin had been head of the opposition; now he may have hoped Dayan was the right man to carry out his own vision of a 'Greater Israel' that would reach at least to the River Jordan. The decisive influence was that of Eshkol's principal coalition partner, Justice Minister Moshe Haim Shapira. Shapira led the National Religious Party, a party that, from 1977, has always marked Israel's extreme right, supporting the settlers in the Occupied Territories and calling for more extreme measures against the Palestinians. However, at that time its views were moderate; Shapira himself was the most dovish minister in the cabinet. His reason for preferring Dayan to Allon was precisely because he hoped the former would *prevent* war.

On the first day of June, having been hounded almost to death, Eshkol capitulated. Not only did he surrender the defence portfolio to Dayan, but he also brought in Begin and one of his supporters. The outcome was a national unity government; more important, whereas previously the cabinet had been evenly split, the new appointments made sure that there would be a majority in favour of war. If, as seems likely, Dayan realized that he owed his appointment to his ability to represent all things to all people, he was very careful not to say so in public. Later he wrote that it had taken 80,000 Egyptian troops to overcome the politicians' antipathy towards him.

A few days earlier General Ezer Weizman, who at that time was chief of the General Staff Division of the General Staff (and who also happened to be married to Ruth's sister, Reuma) had told Eshkol that the IDF was perfectly able to win the war without Dayan. Certainly there is some justification for this argument; neither an army nor its operational plans can be improvised in a few days. It is also true, however, that most cabinet ministers were only too delighted to have what some called 'a natural authority in defence-related matters' to do their thinking for them. Even Rabin looked as if he had a heavy burden taken off his shoulders. To be sure, the new arrangement represented a demotion for him. On the other hand it shielded him from the cabinet, saving him from endless meetings and enabling him to concentrate on his work.

If Dayan's appointment struck the General Staff 'like a fresh wind' (Ariel Sharon),[77] its most important effect was on public opinion. Right or wrong, the Israeli people had come to see Eshkol as elderly, weak and confused, and it greeted the new Minister of Defence with a deep sigh of relief. Some weeks later Dosh, Israel's best known caricaturist, portrayed the situation: in the face of the world, which was waving a question mark, there rose Moshe Dayan in the form of an exclamation mark. Though nothing was said officially, his appointment ended all doubts. Israel would do what had to be done to break the iron ring Nasser had forged around its neck – whatever that might be.

It remained only to make final preparations. Previously there had been a variety of plans. Some provided for the occupation of the Gaza Strip, others for a limited strike into the Sinai, others still for an attack on the Straits of Tyran with the objective of reopening them to Israeli shipping. Dayan, who had reviewed them with the Commander of Southern Front, General Yeshayahu Gavish, thought none of them any good; even if they resulted in the capture of territory, they would leave the bulk of the Egyptian forces, their armour in particular, intact. As in 1956, the objective was to smash the Egyptian armed forces. As in 1956 this could only be achieved by a full-scale war and a deep penetration into the Sinai. The difference was that Israel had no allies with whom to intrigue, so the campaign would proceed in the normal way, i.e. from east to west, the lead taken by the armoured corps rather than the paratroopers. Having ordered Rabin and Gavish to make the necessary changes, Dayan also told them that he did not want the IDF to seize the Suez Canal; this time his objections were based on his fear of the international complications that might follow. So strong was the IDF that, having allocated ten brigades (three *ugdas* and two independent brigades) to the Egyptian front, it still had enough forces left to guard against a Jordanian and/or Syrian attack. At the same time he prohibited any offensive action against Syria and Jordan – not even small land grabs, as Dayan told Rabin.

Late in the afternoon of 3 June 1967 the head of Mossad, General (ret.) Meir Amit, returned from Washington, DC, and drove straight to Jerusalem. He brought the news that the Americans had no objection to Israel going to war, provided they won quickly; the final decision to do so was made the next evening. The weekend had been relatively quiet. To maintain the illusion of calm, thousands of reservists were put on leave and could be seen disporting themselves on the beaches of Tel Aviv. On 4 June Dayan personally contributed to the deception by addressing two hundred representatives of the media. Appearing relaxed and making full use of his sense of humour, he talked to them in soothing terms. He said that the government's policy was to seek a diplomatic solution to the crisis and that he personally agreed with that policy; Israel, he added, did not face developments stopwatch in hand. One journalist, Winston Churchill Jr., he encouraged to return home, telling him that nothing much was going to happen anyhow. Later he claimed that he did not feel quite at ease about this; but consoled himself with the thought that the young man had asked for it by asking him, Dayan, if and when the campaign would start. So persuasive did he appear that the newly appointed US Ambassador to Cairo decided to take the day off.[78] To mislead Arab Intelligence, reports were published that Israeli children would soon start visiting their daddies in the army. As so often before, Dayan's unique ability to cover his guile with a gloss of frankness served him well. This time it did the same for his country.

The Israeli strike, which started at 0745 hours on Monday, 5 June, did indeed take the Egyptians totally by surprise. In his memoirs Dayan says he spent the last hour of peace breakfasting with Rahel, his main mistress during the preceding twelve years, whom we shall meet again later in this chapter. This may not have been the strict truth; a student of mine, who claims to have been present, has told me it was another woman. From the restaurant he drove straight to Air Force Headquarters just a few minutes away. There, he took his place with Rabin and several others on a bench behind the chair on which General Mordechai Hod, commander of the air force, was seated. Since the attack was carried out under cover of absolute radio silence, for the first thirty minutes or so there was nothing to be seen or heard. Then, suddenly, the silence was shattered as the first reports of success came in. There were discreet signs of joy, but the calm was not disturbed; years of discipline, hard work and secretiveness had taught these men how to keep quiet. From then they watched as Hod, drinking vast quantities of water, directed the battle with cool, deliberate precision.

Just at the time when the first wave of aircraft hit their targets – Egyptian airfields – all along the Israeli–Egyptian border the troops of three *ugda*s threw off their camouflage nets, mounted their vehicles, and stormed forward in an enormous cloud of dust. This time the attack proceeded not from south to north, as in 1956, but from north to south; the centre of gravity was at Rafah and El Arish where the most powerful Egyptian forces were concentrated. For the moment, Dayan remained in Tel Aviv. First he addressed the troops on the radio, telling them that the fate of Israel was in their hands. Along with Eshkol and Rabin, he spent the next few hours trying to keep Jordan out of the war, using the head of the UN mission, the Swedish General Odd Bull, to inform King Hussein that Israel would not gratuitously attack his kingdom. It was, however, to no avail. Misled by Nasser about imaginary Egyptian successes against the IDF – at one point, he was told that 75 per cent of the Israeli Air Force had been destroyed – Hussein ordered his forces to strike at Israel by land and by air. At 1230 hours Eshkol, Dayan and Rabin made the decision to fire back. Originally it had been intended to make only minor conquests along Israel's border with Jordan, including some slices of territory in the north of the West Bank (where the Jordanian Army had been shelling an Israeli military airfield) and the Latrun salient that blocked the most direct road to Jerusalem. Late that evening, though, it turned out that progress had been much faster than expected; and Dayan, who until then had only thought of a limited war against Jordan, gave his commanders permission to proceed.

It remained to decide on the continuation of operations against Egypt. In spite of great confusion, the attack on Rafah had gone well. That night in the Sinai, forces belonging to the IDF's northern *ugda* had entered El Arish; others were on their way to the vital crossing at Jebel Libni. Further south, at Abu Agheila, another *ugda*, commanded by Sharon, was launching an attack on the powerful Egyptian fortifications there. In a meeting with Eshkol at 0130 hours on 6 June the continuation of the campaign was discussed. It was agreed that, the next day, the first priority would be the destruction of the Egyptian armour, the second, the occupation of the straits. As for Jordan, Dayan had already permitted local commanders to take out of Eshkol's hands the decision of whether to proceed. Only with regard to the Syrian Army, which up to that point had shelled the Israeli settlements in the Upper Jordan valley but had not left its positions on the Golan Heights, would the IDF remain on the defensive.

Six hours later, still in Tel Aviv, Dayan met with Rabin and the General Staff. By this time Abu Agheila had fallen and the road into the centre of the Sinai was wide open. Rabin wanted to focus on the destruction of the Egyptian armour there, arguing that it would cause the straits to fall by themselves; Dayan, who was worried lest international pressure compel Israel to stop the campaign before its objectives were fully accomplished, insisted that their capture be given priority. He also told Rabin to see to it that the IDF did not go all the way to the Suez Canal but kept 7–10 miles to the east of it.

Around noon on 6 June he paid a brief visit to Jerusalem to see Mount Scopus, which had been an enclave in Jordanian territory since 1948 and had been captured during the previous night. He instructed the local commanders to surround the Old City but not to enter it yet. Next he returned to Tel Aviv for a meeting with the Cabinet Committee for Defence, which wanted to reverse the decision, causing Dayan to say, in private, that he hoped he would not be the one who would have to order the Holy City to be evacuated. Next, as had happened in 1956, there was the problem of setting up a military government for the Gaza Strip which had fallen that very day. Later that night, the Israelis were informed that the Egyptian Army had been ordered to evacuate the entire eastern half of the Sinai Peninsula. Clearly the campaign, which was now all of two days old, was making very good progress. Still Dayan remained worried lest the Security Council impose a ceasefire before Israel could occupy the straits.

In his own words, 7 June was the decisive day. At 1130 hours he met with Eshkol and the principal cabinet ministers. By that time the Minister of Defence could report that over four hundred enemy aircraft had been destroyed, East Jerusalem occupied, and the Egyptian Army brought to the point of collapse; perhaps no wonder he found the ministers, Eshkol specifically included, changed men. During the so-called 'waiting period' the Prime Minister had been caution itself, vacillating and speaking in favour of postponing the attack in the hope of finding a diplomatic solution to the crisis. Now he and many of the others talked wildly of the 'historic opportunity', insisting that the IDF not only complete the destruction of the Egyptian Army – and plant itself on the canal while doing so – but capture the Old City and assault the Golan Heights as well. Concerning Jerusalem, Dayan gave way. At that meeting and another one held on the following evening, 8 June, however, Dayan did what he could to prevent the war from being extended. He pointed out that the original objective had merely been to destroy the Egyptian Army and reopen the straits. He also argued that Syria, being both weak and relatively far away, was 'not a threat',[79] but found himself in a minority of one. Only the fact that Nasser had still not asked for a ceasefire and that the forces needed to attack Syria were still engaged in the West Bank in particular prevented the decision to attack the Golan Heights from being taken there and then.

Dayan was, indeed, in an odd position. During most of his life he had been a hawk, urging strong action and sometimes, as in 1953–55, using underhand methods to get his way. In the mid 1960s he had criticized the government's policy over Syria, but his position was only known to a few; the crisis of May–June 1967 still found him sticking to his views.

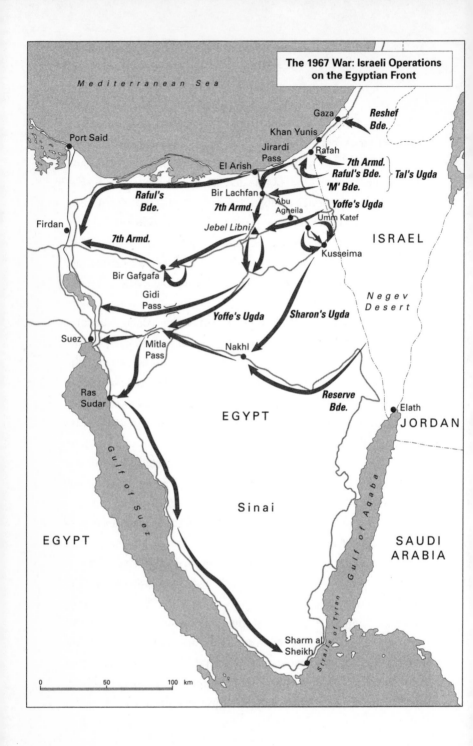

The 1967 War: Israeli Operations on the Egyptian Front

His appointment as Minister of Defence had been due partly to the fact that he was thought to be simultaneously hawkish *and* dovish and partly to his unique standing with public opinion. Now he faced the awkward task of trying to restrain both his colleagues in the cabinet and his subordinates in the General Staff; to no avail. First, local commanders – particularly General David Elazar, Commanding Officer, Northern Front – forced his hand, turning what had started as a limited incursion into the West Bank into a full-scale campaign aimed at evicting the Jordanian Army and occupying much, if not all, of the territory in question. Next he was induced to change his mind about the Old City of Jerusalem, which originally he did not want to enter, and authorize its occupation. Foreseeing that the Gaza Strip with its 250,000 Arab population would spell nothing but trouble he prohibited the IDF from entering it, only to rescind his orders later. Having at one point threatened to court-martial General Yeshayahu Gavish of Southern Command if he permitted his forces to approach the Suez Canal,[80] he later changed his mind on this crucial matter as well.

Most important of all, throughout the week Dayan resisted those who demanded that the IDF respond to Syrian shelling of the Jordan valley settlements by occupying that area; among them was the elderly Prime Minister's young and attractive wife, Miriam, who said she wanted the Golan Heights as her birthday present. During the night he vacillated, receiving conflicting reports on the Syrian Army's strength and morale. He still stuck to his decision at 0600 hours on 9 June, many hours after Egypt had accepted a ceasefire, telling some junior officers of the General Staff that, 'if we strike at the Golan Heights, our hand will hurt.'[81] Within the hour, having consulted neither Eshkol nor Rabin (in his memoirs he says he had tried to reach them but, failing to do so, had taken their consent for granted) he changed his mind. Instead he telephoned Northern Command, asked whether it was ready to move, and ordered the attack to be launched as soon as possible. To add to the paradox, early the same morning Israel's own newspapers reported that the Syrians had proclaimed a unilateral ceasefire and that 'absolute quiet' prevailed along the entire Northern Front.[82]

Why, during this war, he found himself holding back the 'noble steeds' – only to give them free rein at the decisive moment – is anybody's guess. In part, it was the pressure of events. He was worried lest the UN would impose a premature ceasefire; hence all decisions had to be made in great haste and without proper consideration. In part, it must have been his personality. The 1964 clash with Eshkol and the humiliation that followed had left a deep mark; having long recognized his own unsuitability for the top position, there was only so much he could do to stay the hands of his colleagues and, behind them, Israeli public opinion. In part, it was his standing in MAPAI, or lack of it. Though enormously popular with the public, he did not have the party machinery behind him. No man was less suited for, or interested in, the kind of manoeuvring necessary to make one's way in the Byzantine world of Israeli politics; in the end, he represented nobody but himself. As he told his daughter, had he resigned from the cabinet each time he disagreed with its policies he would never have gone anywhere.[83] Still these considerations leave open the question of why he did not take a stronger position with his subordinates when the latter tried to force his hand. In particular, it might have been better for Israel if he had not permitted his order to stay away from the canal to be ignored, given that, in time, the Israeli presence there gave rise to precisely the complications he had expressly foreseen.

Meanwhile, he was literally on top of the world. Though the war had only lasted six days, it ended in a spectacular victory; as Sir Winston Churchill might have said, seldom in history had so few beaten so many, so decisively, in such a short space of time. Eshkol, who was 72 years old and already suffering from the heart condition that was to cause his death

The 1967 War: Israeli Operations on the Jordanian and Syrian Fronts

0   25   50   km

LEBANON

SYRIA

Mount Hermon

Kuneitra

Rafid

Golan

Heights

Nahariya

Safed

Sea of Galilee

Acre

Haifa

Mediterranean Sea

Tiberias

Nazareth

Degania

Tzemach

Mount Gilboa

Beit Shean

Jenin

River Jordan

Tul Karem

Tubias

Kalkiliya

Nablus

Tel Aviv (Jaffa)

Kibiye

S A M A R I A

West Bank

Amman

Damiya Bridge

Beit Choron

Ramallah

Latrun

Jericho

Colonia

Jerusalem

JORDAN

Bethlehem

J U D E A

ISRAEL

Hebron

Gaza Strip

Samua

Dead Sea

Beer Sheva

EGYPT

Dimona

in less than two years, was too elderly, too quintessentially civilian, and too uncharismatic to become the object of public worship. Dayan, in a typical manoeuvre, robbed him of the glory of being the Liberator of Jerusalem. First he told the Prime Minister that the Old City was too dangerous to visit. Then he immediately went there himself, posing in front of the Wailing Wall with Rabin, then chief of staff, and the commander, Central Front, at his side. At 45 years of age, Rabin still looked like a wide-eyed boy from the provinces. Though possessed of a first-class analytical mind, he had never been able to stand up to Dayan and was introverted almost to the point of autism. Nor did he have the quick sense of humour that made up so much of Dayan's charm; compared to the latter he appeared insecure and ill at ease.

As a result, between 1–10 June Dayan was the only Israeli to have his picture displayed in the London *Times*. In the same month his face, whether grim or smiling, adorned the covers of both *Time* and *Newsweek*. Back at home, he was being compared to none other than the Lawgiver; 'from Moses to Moses there was none like Moses', as the saying went. His eyepatch, as well as his aura of sexual availability, helped. According to the London *Daily Mirror*,[84] in Paris 'some of the mam'selles dedicated to being in fashion at all costs' adopted the eyepatch; London and Tokyo experienced a similar craze. The adulation was almost more than a man could stand, to the point where, with his heavy body, he was voted the sexiest man in the world. The cry of '*Ya'ish*' (long live) Dayan' could even be heard from some Arab prisoners of war, although perhaps this was because they hoped it might secure them better treatment. It is very likely that his was the only Israeli name they knew.

While all around him Israel was drunk with victory Dayan reviewed the first position papers concerning the future of the territories Israel had occupied or was soon to occupy. Initially it seems as if, in return for peace, he was prepared to hand back practically the entire Sinai and

Golan Heights to their owners; paradoxically, given that they were largely uninhabited, these were also the easiest territories to hold. The problem of the West Bank was entirely different. Unlike many Israelis, he sympathized with the plight of the refugees streaming east and when the army ambushed some of those trying to return he criticized the practice as inhumane and ordered it to stop. Along with many other Israelis, he considered that Israel had a rightful claim to the West Bank. He intended to retain it; it was not, however, clear how this was to be done. As Dayan well understood, militarily speaking the important line was the watershed running south to north through the mountains of Judea and Samaria. As his fellow ministers well understood, the area on both sides of the watershed was the most heavily inhabited one, containing as many as 80 per cent of the population. In time Israel's wish to defend itself from the east – in particular, the possibility that the Iraqi Army might once again join the Jordanians, as it had done in 1948 and had tried to do again in 1967 – led to the so-called Allon plan. This called for a withdrawal from the entire West Bank except the Jordan valley and a corridor leading to it. Compared to Dayan's plan, it had the advantage that the areas in question were practically empty.

Partly because no Arab country gave a clear signal of being ready to make peace with Israel, partly because the Israelis themselves could not make up their minds as to which parts of the Occupied Territories to keep and which to return, nothing came of these or other proposals. In the absence of a clear policy from above, the situation was dictated by pressures from below. Some came from the settlements in the Upper Jordan valley. After years of being shelled they had just come out from under the Syrian guns; supported by Deputy Prime Minister Allon, who himself came from that district, they wanted the Golan Heights settled in order to make sure it would never be returned to Damascus. Some came from the IDF which claimed, not without justification, that the Suez

Canal represented 'the best anti-tank ditch in the world' and that giving it up without a peace agreement – some would say, even with a peace agreement – was utter folly. As for the West Bank – minus East Jerusalem, which was annexed – this presented the most difficult problem of all. Not only did it contain religious sites such as Hebron, Bethlehem, and others, which were so intimately linked with Jewish history that giving it up appeared like sacrilege to a large part of the population, but such was its strategic importance that even moderate Israelis agreed that retreating from it meant a return to 'the borders of Auschwitz' (Abba Eban).

More by default than by design, Dayan and the ministry he headed assumed the task of governing the Occupied Territories. His first move was to make them secure for Israel. During the first weeks alone the Secret Service killed or imprisoned hundreds of people considered to be PLO sympathizers and, therefore, potential terrorists. Later, in response to terrorist acts, his troops put entire areas under curfew, conducted house-to-house searches, carried out arrests, expelled suspects, and blew up houses. To reinforce the IDF's stranglehold, whole networks of positions were gradually occupied, bases built, roads constructed, water pipes, power lines and telecommunications established. However, as long as he remained Minister of Defence there was no question of a massive influx of Jewish settlers. As for the bulk of population, it had to know who was boss. Still, Dayan's overriding idea was to leave the people in control of their own lives – in his own words, to allow them 'to be born, live and die without ever having to meet an Israeli official'.[85] His objective was to prevent unnecessary friction; in a typical flash of humour, he once said that having to suffer under Israeli bureaucracy was something the Palestinians had done nothing to deserve.

Under his supervision, no attempt was made to change the administration, including that of the Holy Places in Jerusalem – he personally had ordered that no heavy weapons were to be used when Israel's forces entered the Old City – Hebron, and elsewhere. They were left in the hands of the Arab Foundations that had controlled them for hundreds of years; the only changes were those made in order to ensure that non-Moslems, too, could visit them. Elsewhere, too, the principal officials and notables remained at their posts. He personally took to visiting them in their homes, sitting cross-legged, sipping coffee, talking to them, making notes for the future and taking note of any complaints. Aware that the West Bank derived much of its income from exporting agricultural and industrial products to the lands east of the Jordan, he instituted a policy of 'open bridges' to enable commerce to continue. Finally, ignoring protests from his colleagues in the government who worried about the security risk involved, Dayan decided to give both Jews and Arabs complete freedom to cross the border. It was a freedom of which both sides made much use. During the early years after 1967 hundreds of thousands of Jews visited the territories as tourists, sightseeing and bargain-hunting. Equally large numbers of Arabs entered what was now known as 'Old' Israel; whether to find work or walk on the beach for the first time.

Seen in retrospect, such policies could do no more than postpone the problem. To his credit, Dayan realized this; asked how long he thought they would work, he answered that they would do so for a period of 'between two and four years'.[86] In the event, in spite of occasional acts of resistance that started almost immediately and some differences between the West Bank and the Gaza Strip, this proved a gross underestimate. Relative calm prevailed for a much longer period, certainly into the mid 1980s; by enabling the Israelis (Dayan among them) to pretend that all was well, this only made things worse. In part, Palestinian acquiescence was due to the oppressive nature of Egyptian and Jordanian rule. To make the inhabitants of the West Bank pay taxes, King Hussein at one point had resorted to bombarding their homes with artillery; as to Gaza, not only had it been under Egyptian military government but, through-out the years that this government lasted, it remained under night curfew. Compared to this, the Israelis at first appeared if not actually as liberators, then at any rate as a force that did not deliberately set out to abuse the population. What is more, Israel at this time enjoyed an unprecedented boom as economic growth resumed and accelerated even faster than it had before 1965. The boom spilled over into the Occupied Territories. It flooded them with Israeli products, enabled tens of thousands to find work in Israel, and brought in tourists by the hundreds of thousands. As a symbol of the times, the bands of half-naked, barefooted Arab children who infested Jerusalem begging for *bakhshish* (a handout) disappeared. To this day, in spite of everything, they have not returned.

The task of running the territories apart – subject only to the cabinet's directives, which were general and fairly far between, he was their *de facto* ruler – Dayan was kept busy by the need to defend Israel against renewed attacks. Between 1967 and the next major war, which broke out in 1973, there were hundreds if not thousands of incidents. They ranged all the way from the mine planted on a patrol road along the new border with Jordan, to an occasional shooting; and from artillery bombard-ments across the border to an El Al aircraft that was hijacked, taken to Algeria, and released only after Israel set free some captured Palestinian terrorists. As Minister of Defence, it was not Dayan's task to involve him-self in every skirmish, but it *was* his task to lay down policy guidelines and approve each major move, particularly those that might have political repercussions: such as, for example, before a major raid was launched into Jordan (its objective was to capture Yasser Arafat) in 1968; and such as when another raid by Israeli troops blew up thirteen Arab aircraft at Beirut international airport in 1969. In between these and other decisions – as we shall see, he was trying to negotiate some kind of agreement with one or more of Israel's enemies – Dayan remained determined to see for himself as much as possible. For example, he would join a platoon in mounting an ambush along the Jordan River, spending the night lying in a ditch without making the slightest sound or movement, as if he were still a young infantryman. Whatever else may be said of him, no commander ever took greater care to make sure he knew exactly what his subordinates were up against. Which, of course, is one reason why they followed where he led.

In the midst of this he suffered a serious accident. On 21 March 1968 he had gone to a site, not far from Tel Aviv, where sand was being dug for building purposes. He had a young acquaintance whose job was to alert him in case archaeological remains were found at such sites and who had done precisely that. Dayan was just looking into a 5,500-year-old cave laid bare by the bulldozers when it collapsed, all but burying him; as he later wrote, he could not move, he could not breathe, and he thought this was the end. Instead he was dug out and taken to hospital where it was found that his spine had been hurt and one of his vocal cords severed. During his convalescence he was visited not only by Israeli notables but by Arab ones, too, a tribute that would have been inconceivable today. Several months passed before the plastic casing that enclosed the upper part of his body could be removed, and learning how to talk with just one vocal cord took even longer. He tried to put a brave face on it and refused to take painkillers (says he) or stuffed himself with them (says his daughter). Whatever the truth of this, from that time on he was never completely well again.

Although there were incidents along every border – including one in 1968 with Lebanon, which was turning into a base for terrorists – the most dangerous developments by far took place in the south. Of all the Arab countries Egypt had always been the most powerful. Thanks largely to massive Soviet assistance, including, at peak, no fewer than 20,000 advisers who were integrated into every echelon from battalion upwards,

Egypt's recovery from defeat was astonishingly swift. By the end of 1968 its armed forces had been more than rebuilt, quantitatively speaking, although training and, above all, restoring confidence took longer. The situation was made even more difficult by the fact that, immediately after the 1967 War, France, which had long been Israel's main source of arms, imposed an embargo. In time, the French equipment was replaced partly by Israeli-manufactured weapons and partly by American ones which were more plentiful and more advanced than either. Meanwhile the situation of the all-important air force in particular was very difficult and must have given Dayan many an anxious moment. This was all the more so because the Americans played a game of cat and mouse with Israel, trying to link the question of resupply with some kind of control over the latter's nuclear programme.

Though Nasser had accepted a ceasefire on 8 June 1967, the line that now separated Israel from Egypt was seldom entirely quiet. In October 1967 there was a major incident as Egyptian missile-boats sunk an Israeli navy destroyer that had ventured too close to Port Said. In response to that attack, in which the IDF suffered forty-seven sailors dead or missing, Dayan ordered the shelling of the oil-refineries along the Suez Canal, causing damage amounting to hundreds of millions of dollars. Not long afterwards he was quoted as saying that the only 'burning' issue in the Middle East was Egyptian oil; a statement which some found arrogant and unnecessarily offensive. Another round of serious incidents took place in September–October 1968 when, in a series of artillery bombardments and commando raids along the canal, twenty-five Israeli soldiers were killed. This time Dayan and General Staff – it was now headed by Haim Bar Lev, Rabin having left office at the end of 1967 – responded by mounting heliborne raids deep into Egyptian territory. The raids were carefully planned and brilliantly executed, yet they caused few casualties and inflicted relatively little damage. What they did do was demonstrate to Nasser that the whole of his country was exposed. The shock must have been considerable, for over the next four months the front remained quiet.

By this time, the writing was on the wall. From Nasser's point of view, the attempts to pressure Israel into relinquishing the Sinai on his terms – that is, without direct negotiations, without recognition and without peace – had failed. From Israel's point of view, preparations had to be made to defend the area not just against occasional bombardments and raids but against something much more serious. Inside the General Staff, opinions on how this was to be done were divided. One school of thought was represented by Sharon, who was then chief of training, and by the head of the armoured corps, General Israel Tal. In their view, sitting on the canal would merely turn the IDF into a target for the formidable Egyptian artillery; they therefore proposed a mobile defence based on the hills 20 miles or so to the east. Others, headed by the chief of staff, believed that a physical presence on the water line was essential. In its absence the Egyptians might make real gains; first crossing the canal with small forces and then, by asking the Security Council to impose a ceasefire, consolidating their gains before the IDF could eject them. In the end, it was the second solution that prevailed. Writing his memoirs after the 'Bar Lev Line' had fallen in the 1973 War, Dayan mentioned the debate without saying which side he supported; those who wish can see this as a typical attempt on his part to avoid responsibility.

Even as the bulldozers were working day and night to fortify the canal, in February 1969 Eshkol died. Dayan was the second man in the state and the most popular by far. In September 1968, a petition to make him Prime Minister gathered 150,000 signatures within a single week; but he, by saying he was not a candidate, killed the movement almost before it started. Instead, Eshkol's successor was Ms Golda Meir. At the time she was serving as MAPAI secretary-general, a post that identified her with everything that was unsavoury in Israeli politics. She herself had once called her own party leadership 'Tammany Hall' after the infamous New York premises where corrupt officials cut deals and decided elections before they took place. At first she was rather unpopular, but later the iron nerve she displayed in resisting all pressures that Israel surrender the territory it had captured caused her ratings to soar. Her formidable personality apart, she had the party machinery solidly behind her. In her relationship with Dayan it was almost always she who called the shots. He on his part wrote that they were able to work well together. However, they never developed the kind of intimacy and mutual admiration he had enjoyed when his superior had been Ben Gurion.

In April 1969 a thousand Egyptian guns opened fire across the canal and the so-called War of Attrition began. Israeli fortifications proved quite effective in protecting the troops inside; however, the convoys that kept them supplied, the patrols that ran between them, and the lookouts who watched for signs of an Egyptian attempt to cross it were exposed and suffered casualties. In the summer, having consulted Ms Meir and General Bar Lev, Dayan escalated the conflict. The Israeli Air Force was called in and began serving as flying artillery; meanwhile, the IDF also started mounting raids deep into Egyptian territory. Almost all the raids were brilliantly planned and executed, making much of the world hold its breath in admiration. Even so, and even though the Israeli fighters shot down many of the enemy ones sent to intercept them, the Egyptians kept coming. And behind them there loomed the heavy shadow of the Soviet Union, whose own troops took a growing part in the fighting.

In January 1970 it was decided to escalate the conflict still further. Israel had now received a number of F-4 Phantom fighter-bombers from the USA. They were powerful aircraft, capable of carrying more bombs to a greater distance than any other model previously in the IDF's inventory. Flying one way, they even had the range to reach southern USSR; useful for carrying one of the nuclear weapons which, according to foreign sources, Israel had now developed. The main proponent of engaging in 'strategic' bombing was not Dayan but Rabin, who was then serving as ambassador in Washington, DC. Rabin's goal was to bring down Nasser by showing the Egyptian people that their entire country was wide open to attack. He also claimed that the Americans had no objection to the idea and did, in fact, welcome it as a means to make the Soviet Union put pressure on Egypt to accept a ceasefire.[87] Judging from his memoirs, Dayan's task was to explain this plan to the Ministerial Committee on Defence.

In the event, the new strategy was a complete failure. Powerful as the Phantoms were, Israel did not have enough of them to inflict more than pinpricks on its Egyptian enemy. Some of the bombs went astray, one even hitting a school and causing dozens of casualties. Worse still Nasser, instead of losing power or throwing in the sponge, went to Moscow and told Secretary-General Leonid Brezhnev that he might have to capitulate – not to the Israelis but to the Americans – if the USSR did not support him.[88] The loss of a major ally was something the USSR could not afford, and the upshot of the meeting was that Soviet aid to Egypt was greatly increased. More Soviet personnel arrived and gradually built the most up-to-date, most powerful anti-aircraft system in the whole of history up to then. Since Egypt was suffering from an acute shortage of pilots, Soviet ones also began to fly patrols in the skies west of the canal.

The most difficult period was April–May 1970. In spite of the bombs raining down on them, the Soviet–Egyptian defences were not only beginning to bring down Israeli aircraft but were pressing closer to the canal, threatening to deny that area to the Israeli Air Force. Even worse, there were clashes with Soviet-flown fighters and five of these were shot down. This raised the spectre of Soviet intervention; whether the USA would present an adequate counterweight was anybody's guess. In the end it was diplomatic contacts between Washington, Moscow, Cairo and Tel Aviv that saved the situation. On 4 August Ms Meir announced that her government was accepting Security Council Resolution No. 242, which called for a withdrawal from 'territories' occupied in 1967. This cost her the resignation of the right-wing ministers in her cabinet; still, it did enable Nasser to call a ceasefire that went into effect three days later. The Israeli condition for agreeing to it was that the Egyptians should freeze their anti-aircraft defences along the lines they had reached and not push them forward to the canal, where their slant range would cover the western Sinai too. In the event, no sooner had the guns fallen silent than this promise was broken.

In Israel, some people regarded this outcome as a defeat. They demanded that operations be resumed and the Egyptian missiles forced back; chief of them was General (ret.) Weizman whom we have already met and whom we shall meet again. As was so often the case, Dayan's position in respect to this question is not clear. In his memoirs, Weizman blames his brother-in-law for not agreeing with him. Other sources, on the contrary, claim that Dayan saw things in the same light as Weizman, and apparently even considered the possibility of resigning; in the end, he consoled himself with the belief that, should the Egyptian missiles try to cross the canal, they would easily be thrown back by an IDF armoured counter-attack. Be this as it may, the vast majority of Israelis breathed a deep sigh of relief that the War of Attrition, and the daily casualties it demanded, had come to an end. It was time to take stock. In particular, Dayan wanted to find out whether there was some way of preventing the renewal of hostilities.

The Palestinian Liberation Organization already existed and was already engaging in terrorism against Israeli targets both in Israel and abroad. Still, at that time it had not yet achieved wide international recognition;

nor, being based mainly on the refugee camps outside the Occupied Territories, was it clear that it represented the wishes of the latter's population. Attempts to solve the problem of the West Bank accordingly focused on Jordan and its king, Hussein. Both Dayan and other Israeli leaders used various channels to contact him, from emissaries to letters to personal meetings which, on the king's insistence, had to be kept strictly secret. In the end, since he refused to accept anything less than the entire West Bank including East Jerusalem, the talks led nowhere. This was 1970, and Israelis well remembered the awful days in May 1967 when, surrounded on all sides, it seemed as if the end of the world had come. They found the idea of returning to a situation where their country was only 10 miles wide at its narrowest point inconceivable, and understandably so.

Still, it was necessary to keep the king on his throne – the alternative would have been some Palestinian or pro-Nasserite regime – and to keep the country out of the clutches of either Syria or Iraq. Accordingly, in September 1970, when a Syrian force invaded Jordan to assist the Palestinians there against Hussein, Israel, acting in close concert with the USA, concentrated strong forces in the Beth Shean valley. In this way the IDF threatened the Syrian flank, thus helping the Jordanian Army to beat them back. As important, Hussein was left free to deal with the troops of the Palestinian Liberation Organization who threatened his regime. This he did, killing thousands; such was the brutality with which he proceeded that some PLO members preferred to escape to Israel rather than entrust themselves to the tender mercies of their Arab brethren.

As far as may be gleaned from the available evidence, Dayan neither opposed the aid to Jordan – as Ariel Sharon, who wanted Hussein overthrown in order to turn Jordan into a Palestinian state, did – nor supported it. Possibly his silence indicates that he did not agree with the policy actually adopted and that he was already beginning to lose influence. More and more during these days, it was Ms Meir, Allon (as deputy Prime Minister), General Bar Lev and Rabin who made the decisions. Allon, in particular, was a bitter rival. His enmity with Dayan dated back to the time when he was the adored commander of PALMACH – his men worshipped him as if he were God – and Dayan the wounded outsider. In having him at her elbow, Ms Meir must have known that he was certain to oppose anything her Minister of Defence might say or do.

While this episode ended well for Israel, bringing it closer to the USA than perhaps at any time before or since, Dayan's inability to bring negotiations with Egypt to a successful conclusion had more fateful consequences. As will be remembered, just before the 1967 War he had opposed an Israeli approach to the Suez Canal, arguing that its presence there would constitute an intolerable challenge to the Egyptians as well as leading to international complications. As will also be remembered, his advice was not followed as Israeli units did reach the canal and dug in there; when the time came, either he was unable to recall them or he had changed his mind. The upshot was the War of Attrition that cost Israel hundreds of dead, most of them killed not inside the fortifications but on the way to or from them – for the sake of a fresh supply of tomatoes, as one retired general turned critic put it. For all the hyperbole about 'the world's best anti-tank ditch', sitting directly under an artillery force that consisted of over a thousand barrels was not the most comfortable situation imaginable; the more so because, however bad it might be in other ways, such as conducting manoeuvre warfare, artillery had always been the Egyptian Army's strong point.

In September 1970 Nasser died, bringing to power Anwar Sadat. To Dayan, the time appeared ripe for negotiation. He proposed to withdraw the Israeli forces from the canal, which had been closed since 1967. In return, the Egyptians would proclaim an end to belligerency; by enabling them to open the canal and rebuild the cities on its eastern bank, Dayan hoped to give them a real stake in keeping the peace. From Sadat's point of view the problem was to make sure that the interim agreement would not turn into a final one, thus forcing Egypt to give up its claim to repossess the entire Sinai. From Israel's point of view, the problem was to ensure that the war would not be resumed after the peninsula's western part had been surrendered, and that the territories it considered vital to its security – the straits above all – should stay in its hands.

The talks lasted about a year and a half. In the end, the opposing objectives proved impossible to reconcile. According to US National Security adviser Henry Kissinger, Dayan was the only member of the Israeli cabinet who was prepared to consider any kind of Egyptian military presence east of the canal; yet at one point even he went on record as saying that 'the Straits [of Tyran] without peace are preferable to peace without the Straits'. If it is true, as has been claimed, that this was a bellicose and arrogant statement, then it reflected the stance of Ms Meir. She opposed any retreat that did not form part of a final peace agreement; one source claims she told her Minister of Defence that his place was in a mental hospital.[89] At the time, confidence in Israel's military power and its ability to defeat the Arabs was widely shared both in Israel and abroad. Faced with this power Sadat, who repeatedly promised to use force to 'liberate' the Sinai and repeatedly put off the date of the attack, was perceived as a clown. If he refused to have the Sinai or part of it back on terms acceptable to Israel, so the common wisdom went, then so much the worse for him.

Compared to the tremendous strain of the previous years, 1971–73 was more or less peaceful. The canal border was absolutely quiet. So was the border with Jordan, which Hussein's army was now policing much more effectively than the IDF ever had. There were skirmishes on the Golan Heights as well as on the Lebanese border; nor were the Occupied

Territories ever free from terrorism. On the whole, though, Israeli rule over the territories could still be considered a great success, confirmed by the hordes of tourists who came to visit them. Neither the border skirmishes nor attacks on Israeli targets abroad involved large numbers of casualties, let alone threatened the country's existence as they seemed to do both in 1967 and at the height of the War of Attrition. The change showed in Israel's defence budget. Even as new weapons continued arriving from the USA, it fell from 24 per cent of GNP in 1971 to 16 per cent in 1973. There were already signs that the economy was overheating, with attendant social strain, yet for most Israelis life was as good as it had ever been.

For Dayan personally these were fairly relaxed, if not entirely happy, years. In December 1971 he was finally divorced. It came about after he had parted from yet another of his young paramours, a Ms Elisheva Zisich. She ran a boutique in Tel Aviv and had written to him for a favour. Intrigued, he asked her to visit him, and the rest followed of itself. As usual, he played her off against the others. At one point Elisheva, Ruth and Rahel were all stalking each other. What he thought of it all is anybody's guess; but it can hardly have increased his respect for the opposite sex. Later, when he tried to get rid of Ms Zisich, her mother turned the table on him by recording their telephone conversations. He must have said something to her that he could not retract. She threatened to sue him for breach of promise; in the end, he had to pay her the equivalent of $3,300. Not content with this, the older Ms Zisich spread the tapes around, so that listening to them became a favourite pastime at parties. This time the humiliation was too great for Ruth. She asked for a divorce which was granted as soon as the details had been settled. By mutual agreement she moved out of their home of almost twenty years while he remained in it. Later she wrote that she had never wanted his fame and felt liberated; yet for decades thereafter she continued to speak about him and write about him. Without question, he remained the love of her life. She did not remarry, and many of his early collaborators still regard her as his 'real' wife.

A year and a half later, he married Rahel Karmon. They had met in 1955 when they had accidentally been seated together on a flight from Rome to Tel Aviv; from there, as he engagingly wrote, they continued on their own steam. Ten years younger than Dayan, Rahel, like Ruth in her time, came from an upper-class background; at the time she was married to a wealthy lawyer. More than Ruth, who had become a true farmer's wife and in her home walked about barefoot, she had style. In 1958 she divorced her husband and went to live alone with her two children. During the mid 1960s Dayan employed her as his secretary in the fishing company he directed. The fact that she was his great love did not prevent him from carrying on with other women. Sometimes he talked to her on the phone from his Zahala home. With Ruth within earshot, he would tell her not to worry about her competitors; when it came to making his women fight with each other he had no peer. Still, during the weeks when he lay wounded in hospital, it had been Rahel who visited him at night when everybody else had left.

She had class, and her lifestyle was expensive. As he himself put it proudly, he surrounded her with luxuries 'as in the movies'.[90] This was a kind of life which Ruth, who had left her rich parents' home in order to share in the Spartan life of Nahalal, had never wanted. In order to accommodate it, the bedrooms in which his children had once lived had to be modified or demolished; not surprisingly, they took it badly. Rahel in turn saw to it that he should look after himself, acting, as Yael put it, as the fairy-tale princess who had kissed the rough, sometimes almost uncouth, frog from Nahalal. The open shirts and khaki pants he had previously favoured disappeared, their place being taken by expensive suits and high-quality sweaters. Previously he had gulped down his food, the less pretentious the better. Now he became something of a gourmet, and at one point was even elected a Knight of a club called 'The International Order of the Grill'. Their combined expensive tastes may have had something to do with his fascination with money, which was turning into an obsession. During the last years of his life he was charging people for anything he did or did not do including autographs, photographs, interviews, and, indirectly, his very presence at this gathering or that. At the same time, he totally lost any interest in other women.

In the aftermath of the 1967 War Dayan was at the peak of his glory and subject to the kind of adulation that could easily turn anyone's mind. Six years later, after some very difficult trials and countless twists and turns, his reputation was still almost as high as ever. In his domestic life, and in spite of his impaired health, he had finally found happiness, or at least as much of it as he was capable of. His happiness may have had something to do with the fact that Rahel, unlike Ruth, never developed into a public personality in her own right. Once during the 1970s she was asked whether she had influenced him when he voted in favour of a law concerning equal opportunity for women. She answered that 'Moshe' was quite capable of making up his own mind. It was a clever answer by a clever woman. In his entire life, the one thing he could least stand was fools. The older he grew, the more true this became.

In political life, he was already beginning to lose influence as Ms Meir favoured other advisers. In addition to those mentioned above, they included a veteran politician, Israel Galili. Until March 1948, when Ben Gurion fired him, Galili had been commander-in-chief of Hagana. Later he took up the role of elder politician and headed the left-wing coalition party of which Allon was also a member; most important of all, he enjoyed the personal favour of Ms Meir. Dayan's waning influence was most evident when she refused to bring the negotiations with Egypt, of which he was the principal architect, to a successful end. This was clearly a defeat for him, albeit one which, under the circumstances, may have been unavoidable; as he later put it, he had failed to convince his colleagues that a reopened Suez Canal constituted a better guarantee against attack than did the Bar Lev Line. Another sign of decline was the fact that she rejected Dayan's candidate for chief of staff. Instead she selected Elazar, the same general who had helped force Dayan's hand both with regard to occupying the West Bank and in the decision to assault the Golan Heights. If, as has been claimed, Ms Meir was under Dayan's spell, then this was a strange way of showing it. Yet at the time these problems were only known to a few in Israel or abroad. Come the summer of 1973, however, and Dayan had some reason to consider the future with confidence.

CHAPTER 6

October Earthquake

At the beginning of 1973 Moshe Dayan was 57 years old. Thirty-six years had passed since he first joined Hagana. The youth who had once guided British units in their efforts to secure the oil pipeline near Nahalal was now in charge of one of the most highly regarded war-machines the world had ever seen, including 350,000 troops, six to seven divisions, over 2,000 tanks and some 400 combat aircraft. Since 1967 both the land and air forces had grown by over 50 per cent. More important still, new weapons had taken the place of the old, leading to a dramatic rise in the amount of firepower that could be brought to bear by the air force and navy in particular.

On the other side of Israel's border the concentration of Arab forces was even larger. Egypt and Syria, Israel's main opponents, were capable of fielding approximately 4,000 tanks and 700 combat aircraft; to these should be added Iraqi forces (Iraq participated in both the 1948 and 1967 wars), those of Jordan, and various smaller contingents sent by other Arab states as far away as Morocco. Added to this was the fact that Egyptian and Syrian forces in particular consisted of regulars. Unlike the IDF, some three-quarters of which were made up of reservists who had to be called up before they could be thrown into action, these armies could attack without having to mobilize or redeploy. As a result, advance warning concerning their intentions was much harder to obtain; and the possible consequences of failing to do so, all the more severe.

Along with the rest of the General Staff, Dayan watched the Arab build-up very closely, receiving daily reports from sources that ranged from direct observation to spies occupying senior positions in the Syrian government. He was, however, dependent on Military Intelligence, whose chief, General Eliyahu Zeira, was convinced there would be no war. Between December 1972 and April 1973 Israel's top political and military leaders met regularly. Neither Dayan nor General Elazar contented themselves with receiving their subordinates' reports, but insisted on reading 'raw' intelligence in order to make up their own minds. Each time Dayan would tell his colleagues that the Arabs, the Egyptians in particular, seemed to be 'rolling towards war'[91] – to quote one of the expressions he used. Each time Zeira answered that there were no immediate signs of an attack, and that he considered the probability of one to be very low. He was convinced that he would be able to identify an eventual Egyptian crossing 'a few days ahead of time'. As for the Syrians, he expected them to join in only later.[92]

As an academic exercise, engaging in guesswork is easy and even entertaining. In the real world, such guesswork may have important consequences and indeed a wrong guess might well put the country in danger or, at the very least, lead to numerous unnecessary casualties. It was on the basis of their conclusions that the group, with Dayan at its head, had to decide whether to alert Ms Meir; whether to tell the public, thus possibly leading to a panic which might turn out to be unjustified and damage the prestige of the army they were leading; and whether to declare a state of readiness, such as calling up reservists. At least once a warning was passed to Kissinger so that he might inform the Egyptians that the Israelis knew of their plans and were ready for them. The objective was to prevent the attack taking place; there was, however, a limit to the number of times one could cry 'wolf' and still expect Washington to pay attention. The most serious warnings were given in late April. Various dates – 1 May, 7 May, 2 June – were mentioned. As a precaution, Dayan ordered partial mobilization; along with the air force, which was to act as flying artillery, the 515 tanks now deployed on both fronts were supposed to be capable of repelling a combined Egyptian–Syrian attack or at least containing it until the reserves arrived.

On 21 May Dayan told the General Staff to 'take into account there will be a renewal of the war during the second half of this summer' and prepare to inflict a 'decisive defeat'[93] on Egypt and Syria. The next day he told the Parliamentary Committee for Foreign Affairs and Defence that, contrary to the views of Military Intelligence, the two countries might attack even though they knew they could not reconquer the Occupied Territories; their objective being not military victory but political achievement. In the event, no war materialized – we now know that it had been planned but was postponed – and Zeira appeared to have been vindicated. Beginning in the second half of June the Israeli defence establishment started to breathe more easily. The armoured battalions that had been called up were discharged. In July Dayan told *Time* that he did not foresee a large-scale war during the next decade. On 4 September he told the air force commander that, although political pressures on Israel would probably intensify, he did not expect war to break out in the near future.

Up to this point the emphasis was on the Southern Front, the assumption being that, as in 1967, the Syrians would only go to war after the Egyptians had done so. However, on 13 September there was a clash with the Syrian Air Force in which thirteen Syrian fighters were shot down. Dayan was worried about a possible response, and in a series of meetings did not hide his concern from the General Staff. Still Zeira insisted that no war was imminent. On 26 September he received the support of

Elazar who said that Syria could do 'nothing more idiotic' than to attack on its own. Dayan, too, agreed that a full-scale war was unlikely. Still, he believed that the Syrians would probably do *something*, be it a large-scale raid, or an air attack, or anything else. The same day he went to the Golan Heights in order to see for himself. He met the Commanding Officer, Northern Front, General Hofi, and together they climbed up the local observation posts which were located on top of hills occupied in 1967. Hofi told Dayan that his scouts could look so far into Syria as to rule out a daytime surprise attack. To Dayan's question of whether the Syrians could not put down an artillery barrage from a standing start, he answered that they would first have to remove the camouflage nets from their guns. In the event, he was proved wrong. When the Syrians did take off the nets, the units on the spot had only a few minutes' warning.

Throughout the first week of October the meetings continued. By now there was plenty of evidence – consisting of both direct observation and air photographs – that the Egyptians and Syrians were deploying massive forces along the borders as if in preparation for an attack. Zeira, though, told his colleagues it was all part of an exercise. To the extent that the Egyptians were in fact using their annual exercise to disguise their plans, he was right; and, standing behind Zeira was the chief of staff, General Elazar. On 2 October, Elazar said he 'did not think we are facing a combined Egyptian–Syrian attack'.[94] Technically Dayan, as Minister of Defence, could have overruled them; as Zeira rightly notes,[95] they all had access to the same information. Instead, Dayan merely expressed his anxiety about the 'monstrous' Arab build-up. Perhaps because of his failing health, perhaps because he had been tamed by Ms Meir, at this point in his career overruling people was something he did only rarely.

On 4 October Military Intelligence announced that the Soviets were evacuating the families of troops who were serving as advisers to the Syrian and Egyptian armed forces. The news caused Dayan even greater concern. Had he wanted to, he could have made Elazar do much more than put the IDF put on 'C' alert (the highest alert short of mobilization) and deploy another brigade on the Golan Heights; instead, in a meeting with Ms Meir, he did not disagree with Elazar and Zeira when they argued that there would be no war. After all, the chief of intelligence had proved to be right before. Worse, the accusation that Israel had brought about the 1967 War by threatening to attack Syria still rankled and made Dayan fear the political implications of mobilization. It might, indeed, lead to the very war Israel most wanted to avoid.

Even in retrospect, to allocate responsibility for the 'oversight' that led to the IDF being taken by surprise is not easy. Certainly most Israelis, Dayan and the General Staff included, shared in the overconfidence that resulted from their spectacular victory in the 1967 War; in fact, their feeling that the Arab armies were incompetent and would be easily repulsed was shared as far away as the National Security Council in Washington, DC. Certainly Zeira, and to a lesser extent Elazar, disregarded the many warnings that reached them. It may be true, as has been claimed, that the chief of intelligence himself was misled by subordinates who withheld information from him; if so, it was his own fault. As for Dayan, during the spring he felt less confident than any of his principal subordinates. In the summer he seemed to calm down, but the incident of 13 September revived his anxiety and at one point he even asked Elazar and Zeira whether the exercises the Egyptians were holding might not serve as cover for their plan to attack. In the event he was proved right since *Tahrir* 41, as the exercise was called, was designed to do just what Dayan thought it might. Nevertheless, having received a negative answer, he did not impose his will. Political considerations apart, his authority, together with his health, was already declining.

The warning that finally turned the tables arrived at 0400 hours on 6 October. Even then it was not conclusive: not only had the same source proved wrong before, but even now he gave H-hour as 1800 hours instead of 1400 as it actually was. Nevertheless he was taken seriously, and at 0600 hours Dayan, who had already given orders for the Jewish settlements on the Golan Heights to be evacuated, met with Elazar. At issue was the question of whether the air force should launch a preventive strike, in particular at Syrian missile-defences. Feeling that the political situation was less favourable than in 1967, Dayan refused permission. The two men decided to 'go to Golda' and take their disagreement to the Prime Minister. Despite barely knowing what a division was (as she later admitted),[96] she would also have to rule on whether to mobilize two reserve divisions – as Dayan, who was still thinking in terms of a war against Syria alone, wanted – or four, as Elazar demanded.

The meeting with Ms Meir had to wait until 0800 hours as Elazar wanted first to talk to his generals, who were on their way to the fronts. Thus only six hours, not ten as Dayan and Elazar believed, remained for an eventual preventive strike against the Syrians. In any case, the weather over the Golan was overcast, which allowed only the Syrian airfields, but not the missile batteries, to be attacked; in addition, it has been claimed that the Israelis were unfamiliar with their opponents' new SA6 anti-aircraft missiles and that any attempt to destroy the defences would have failed. In the event Ms Meir ruled out a preventive strike for political reasons. In this she was absolutely right, as Kissinger later told Dayan that, had such a strike been launched, Israel would not have received 'a single nail' in aid.[97] Siding with Elazar, she ordered full mobilization, in which she was also entirely correct. Not that it mattered much, for mobilization arrangements, distances and the condition of the roads meant that no reserve units would be able to reach the front before the war started anyhow. Elazar, though, still did not order the air force commander to change the mission from preventive strike to air superiority with ground support. As a result, when the war started at 1400 hours the aircraft were armed with the wrong munitions and precious time was wasted before they could be reconfigured. To speed the process, some aircraft even took off, dumped their bombs into the sea and returned to reload. Whatever failings the IDF may have had in 1973, a lack of determination was not one of them.

The meeting with Ms Meir over, Dayan questioned Elazar in detail as to the state of Israeli defences and the plans to use them, but did not give any orders. At 1200 there was a cabinet meeting. The issue on the table was whether, in case either Egypt or Syria attacked Israel, the IDF would strike at its other enemy as well. Ms Meir's Minister of the Treasury was Pinhas Sapir, the man who had once clashed with Dayan over tomatoes. He was just complaining about having to make weighty decisions at such short notice when the air-raid sirens started wailing; from now on, all Dayan could do was wait for reports of the fighting to arrive. At 1600 hours he gave a press conference. The dominant impression on that day, created by means of telephone conversations that Dayan and Elazar had with the front commanders, was that the situation on the Golan Heights was tolerable. By contrast, that in the Sinai was going from bad to worse as the fortifications of the Bar Lev Line fell or were surrounded and as the first Israeli counter-attacks were repulsed with heavy loss. Accordingly, in the evening, it was decided to use the air force against the Egyptians first.

From midnight on, the situation changed. Though the border fortifications on the Golan held, the Israeli armoured brigade that was holding the southern part of the Heights came under heavy attack by two Syrian divisions; so heavy, indeed, that it literally did not know what was hitting it. Unlike Elazar, Dayan was not tied to Tel Aviv by the need to run the army. Using his freedom, at 0400 hours he went to visit General Hofi at his headquarters, which were located in the Galilee near Safed, in order to talk to him face to face. What he heard shocked him. The above-mentioned brigade had been all but wiped out, which meant that there was no longer anything standing between the Syrians and the Sea of Galilee; indeed Hofi was already giving orders for the Jordanian bridges to be prepared for demolition. Since Elazar could not be reached, Dayan called the air force commander directly. Using highly charged language, he ordered him to switch aircraft from the Egyptian front, where they were attacking bridges and anti-aircraft defences, to close support missions on the Golan Heights. Much later, the air force commander claimed that suspending the aerial offensive against Egypt had been a mistake and that, had it been allowed to proceed, it would have destroyed the missiles on that front. Even if this claim is correct, it still does not change the fact that Dayan was right in giving priority to saving the Heights. And saved they were, albeit at a very heavy loss in aircraft and pilots.

By 0820 Dayan was back at General Headquarters. Only twenty-four hours earlier he had asked Elazar, in Ms Meir's presence, what he would do with tens of thousands of surplus reservists if no war materialized; now Israel found itself in the worst crisis since the Arab armies had invaded in 1948. Discussing the situation with Elazar – at no point during these days was there any question of giving orders to the chief of staff – he told him that the fortifications along the Suez Canal no longer mattered and that attempts to rescue them might have to cease. Before deciding anything, he flew south to see for himself. The Commanding Officer, Southern Front, was General Shmuel Gonen. In 1967 he had distinguished himself by leading the key armoured brigade that had broken through at Rafah. As Front commander he was new in the job – he had only just taken over from General Sharon – inexperienced, and unable to control his subordinates, two of whom had been his superiors earlier in his career.

What he learnt in the south made him all the more anxious. Though some of the fortifications were still holding out, all were surrounded.

Armed only with light weapons, they were helpless to stop the Egyptian invasion. Trying to rescue them, the IDF was merely frittering away its tanks; they were being met by a hail of anti-tank missiles, and two-thirds of those present in the Sinai at the outbreak of the war had already been lost. Using grim language – 'This is war' – Dayan told Gonen the counter-attacks had to stop and that those troops in the fortifications who had not yet been killed should make their way east as best they could. He also wanted the remaining forces to be withdrawn to the passes some 20 miles east of the canal where they should form a second defensive line. Later there was some controversy as to whether this was 'ministerial advice' or a direct order. In any case it did not matter. The Egyptians were careful not to advance beyond the range of their anti-aircraft missiles, most of which remained west of the canal. Thus, Gonen was able to stabilize his front along a lateral road running approximately 8 miles to the east of the canal.

At 1500 hours on the same day, Sunday, 7 October, Dayan – later joined by Elazar – reported to Ms Meir and the ministerial committee on defence. Surprisingly enough, the Golan Heights were barely mentioned; either those present did not realize how serious the situation there was or else they were confident that the first reserve division, whose advance units were due to arrive in a few hours, would be able to halt the Syrians. Be this as it may, the discussion centred on the Southern Front. Dayan explained that, bad as the IDF's losses were, provided it stopped frittering away its forces it should be able to hold the line. In the meantime, two divisions of reservists were already beginning to join the regular one deployed there. The decision was made to use them to counter-attack the next day. Later that afternoon, Elazar flew to Southern Command to settle the details with Gonen and the divisional commanders.

Throughout this, Dayan's mood was on the sombre side. In 1967, asked about the possibility of the Egyptians launching surface to surface missiles at Israel, he had answered 'let them try'. Now his attempts at jocularity fell flat and he was unable to galvanize either Hofi or Gonen. If anything Elazar and the other officers of the General Staff found him unduly pessimistic. After the war was over, some of them even accused him of speaking about 'the destruction of the Third Temple', a heavily loaded expression with near-apocalyptic overtones. Had he been called upon to justify himself, Dayan would have been able to say that he had visited the front commanders and seen what he had seen. This time there could be no question of the enemy scattering like birds or being 'waved off' across the canal, as some members of the General Staff thought they would be. That same evening he reported to the assembled cabinet. He admitted that he had underestimated the enemy, that the Arab armies were fighting well and that the battles taking place on both fronts had been unexpectedly severe. Still he told Bar Lev, then serving as Minister of Trade and Industry, that provided there were no special blunders or surprises, Israel would gain the upper hand.

The counter-offensive against Egypt was launched on the morning of 8 October, and ended in a complete failure. Two IDF tank battalions were virtually wiped out, the commander of one being captured. In part, this was because of a whole series of misunderstandings between Elazar, Gonen, and the two divisional commanders – one of them Ariel Sharon – who carried out the actual attack. As a result, it was by no means clear who was to do what, on what conditions, and in what order. Besides, the movement was premature and the troops who, forty-eight hours earlier, had still been civilians, were not yet ready with regard particularly to air-support, and to artillery. Dayan's part in this episode, which entered history as the greatest defeat ever suffered by the IDF in a single battle, was minor. He had met Elazar after the latter's return from the Sinai and listened as the chief of staff explained the plan. During the offensive he received reports of its progress. He did not, however, interfere, as

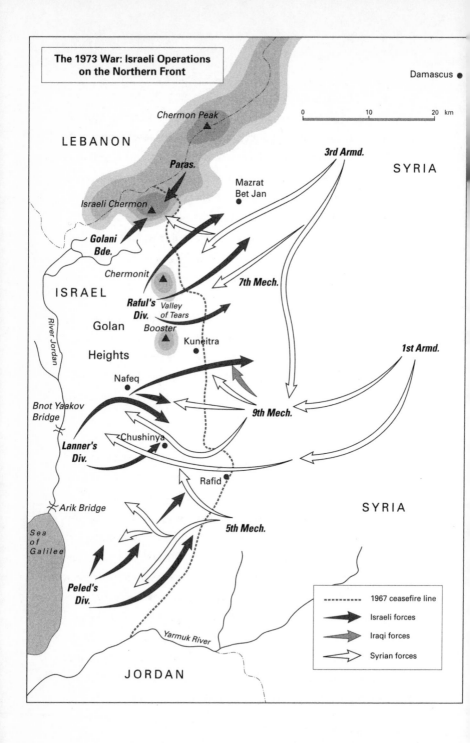

The 1973 War: Israeli Operations on the Northern Front

Damascus

0   10   20 km

Chermon Peak

LEBANON

Paras.

3rd Armd.

SYRIA

Mazrat
Bet Jan

Israeli Chermon

Golani
Bde.

7th Mech.

Chermonit

ISRAEL

Raful's
Div.

Valley
of Tears

Golan

Booster

Kuneitra

1st Armd.

Heights

Nafeq

9th Mech.

River Jordan

Bnot Yaakov
Bridge

Lanner's
Div.

Chushinya

Rafid

SYRIA

Arik Bridge

Sea
of
Galilee

5th Mech.

Peled's
Div.

Yarmuk River

JORDAN

- - - - - - - - - 1967 ceasefire line

Israeli forces

Iraqi forces

Syrian forces

perhaps he should have done. Had he used the night to talk directly to the Commanding Officer, Southern Front, as well as to the divisional commanders in charge, perhaps he would have discovered the extent of the disaster.

That evening, 8 October, was the most difficult in the entire war. In the Sinai, the failure of the Israeli counter-offensive shocked GHQ and left it wondering how it would ever recapture the territory it had lost. There was even talk of asking Washington, DC, to help arrange a ceasefire with the forces standing in place – which, assuming the Egyptians had agreed, would have constituted a clear-cut victory for them. On the Golan Heights, although the situation in the southern part had been stabilized, the Syrians threw in a fresh division in an effort to achieve a breakthrough further to the north. After ferocious fighting throughout the night, the crisis came at around noon. With some of his tanks down to just two rounds, the commander of the brigade defending the area informed his superiors that he was nearing the end of his tether.

According to Dayan's own account, what saved the situation was a young officer named Yossi. When the war broke out Yossi had just been on his honeymoon in Nepal. He flew back to Israel and was given command of an improvised force of fifteen tanks, roughly equal to half an armoured battalion. Proceeding from south to north, he drove into the Syrian rear, causing them to suspend their offensive; judging by the fact that the Syrian rear-units were the first to turn tail, their orders must have come from above. Foreign sources tell the story differently. According to a *Time* article of March 1976, at some time during the night of 8/9 October, Dayan, casting about wildly for anything that might prevent the Syrians from reaching the Jordan valley and the Israeli settlements there, put Israel's nuclear forces on alert. Having done so, he contacted Kissinger and asked him to pass a suitable warning to Damascus.

By the morning of Wednesday, 10 October, the worst crisis was over. On the Golan Heights, the three IDF divisions now operating in the area were completing the encirclement of the Syrian forces that had broken through in the south. Soon they found themselves back on the so-called 'Purple Line' that marked the 1967 ceasefire. That evening, following a six-hour meeting with Ms Meir, Galili, Allon, Elazar, and several others, Dayan ordered an assault on Syria proper. The objective was to inflict a heavy blow on the Syrian Army and to seize territory. The attack took place the next day, bringing the IDF to within artillery-range of Damascus. Meanwhile, in the Sinai, another small Israeli attack had been repulsed on the 9th. However, the Egyptians showed no inclination to exploit their success, thus giving the IDF a much-needed respite.

For Dayan personally, things were settling down into a routine. Earlier than most of his subordinates in the General Staff and also than his colleagues in the cabinet, he had grasped that this was going to be a war and not a repetition of past conflicts in which Arab forces had so often broken and run. Perhaps because he did, after all, symbolize Israeli military power, there were those both in the cabinet and the General Staff who interpreted his attitude as unduly pessimistic, even defeatist. Now dressed in a uniform without insignia and sporting a cap of the kind worn by service-troops in Vietnam, he spent much of his time visiting the fronts. In between he attended meetings with the General Staff and the cabinet – one of his most pressing concerns was to get the United States to supply Israel with new ammunition and fighter bombers to replace its losses and permit the war to continue – and talked to the media. Though his consent was still needed for any major operations, there is no record of any attempt on his side to overrule the chief of staff, who, having mastered the first crisis, was very much in control and running the war as well as anyone could.

By this time most of the economically active male population were away, serving in the army. As a result, the roads were all but empty. Dayan

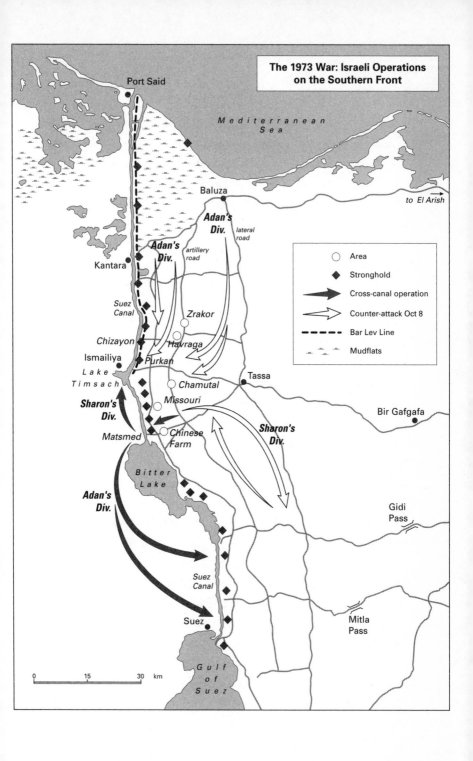

could have driven from GHQ to his Zahala home in about ten minutes; nowadays, with traffic, the same journey would take well over half an hour. In fact there was little point in his doing so. His daughter was working as a volunteer nurse at one of Israel's main hospitals, his two sons were at the front, and Rahel had long held a job in the Israeli equivalent of the PX where she continued to work every day. On the few occasions he did go home he found it eerily quiet; the house, the garden, and even the antiques had not changed and Rahel did what she could to keep everything in place. Still, all appeared to have lost their meaning in face of the tremendous drama going on elsewhere.

On 12 October, with the immediate crisis past, he went to Ms Meir and submitted his resignation. Like everybody else, the Prime Minister was shocked by the suddenness of the Arab onslaught but, having recovered her nerve, she went on to run the war with iron self-control and determination. Although she does not say so in her memoirs, she had been disappointed by Dayan's attitude, blaming him for a pessimism bordering on instability; 'the great Dayan', she is reported to have said, 'goes now one way, now that'. From her perspective, she was undoubtedly right. From his perspective, he was equally right. As we saw, even before the war he had been less confident than his subordinates. As we also saw, he no longer had what was needed to overrule them. This may have been due partly to his declining health, but equally important was the fact that Ms Meir was already shifting her support to Elazar. Behind Elazar stood Galili and Allon, who were thus exercising power but not responsibility. At Ms Meir's request, Galili and Allon were also present at many of her deliberations with Dayan and Elazar. After the war, it was they who spread rumours concerning Dayan's defeatism.

In Dayan's favour it must be said that for all his long-standing tendency to look down on Arab fighting power, he was perhaps the first Israeli leader to realize that this time things were different. Given what had happened, asking the Prime Minister whether she still retained her confidence in him was both fair and vitally important if they were to continue working side by side. She in turn rose to the occasion by refraining from voicing any reservations she may have had and promising him her full support; in her memoirs, she wrote that he never gave her cause to regret her decision. In any case, changing horses in mid campaign is usually a bad idea, the more so when this particular horse had been identified with Israeli military power so completely and for so long that changing him would have a major impact on public opinion in Israel, in the Arab capitals, and in the world at large.

By this time the war was going much better for Israel. Back in Washington, DC, the Americans had finally decided to resupply Israel and an aerial bridge carrying ammunition was being organized. On the Northern Front, the IDF had advanced to within 25 miles of Damascus before coming to a halt. Well realizing that the city was capable of swallowing up any number of IDF troops, Dayan had never wanted to occupy it. He, would, however, have preferred to come closer still; doing so would have allowed the IDF to bring the full weight of its artillery to bear on the city in preparation for the ceasefire talks to come. In the event, visiting the front on 12 October, he could not help but notice how the troops were falling asleep each time the columns halted. Nor was it a question of the rank and file alone. The higher the level of command, the more demoralized they seemed to be. Though he talked to all the important commanders, he could not make them press harder than they did.

In the south, meanwhile, there was a comparative lull that lasted throughout Wednesday, Thursday and Friday. Among the Israeli General Staff there was no doubt that the IDF should go on the offensive on that front too; the only question was whether to do so immediately, or wait until after the Egyptians had launched another attack and exhausted themselves by so doing. In the event Dayan and Elazar, strongly supported by Bar Lev, who had been superimposed over Gonen on 10 October, decided on the second course. Their decision proved right. On Sunday, 14 October, the Egyptians began to advance, moving in line abreast 'like complete idiots', as Gonen told the General Staff.[98] Soon their armour and infantry were met by the well-aimed fire of Israeli tanks entrenched along the hills in the Western Sinai. By the time the day ended, hundreds of 'bonfires' were lighting up the desert which, indeed, had come to resemble a vast slaughterhouse. As Bar Lev told Ms Meir on the telephone that evening, Egyptians and Israelis were both beginning to revert to their accustomed roles, each side in its own way. Sharon, who was commanding one of three Israeli divisions now operating in the Sinai and who had played a major role in beating back the Egyptians, put it more succinctly: 'They came, they were screwed, they ran'.

That evening, the decision to cross the canal was made by Dayan and the General Staff despite the objections of Allon, who had been called in by Ms Meir. Implementing the order was the mission of Bar Lev and the divisional commanders, Generals Sharon and Adan. As always when a decision had been taken and he had nothing better to do, Dayan went to visit the front. The ability to leave his subordinates alone was one of his strong points; at the same time, he wanted to get the true story before it became distorted by going through the chain of command. The first stage of the operation went smoothly as a battalion of paratroopers, using rubber boats, crossed without meeting any opposition on the night of 15/16 October. However, the next two days saw some of the toughest fighting of the entire war. First, the Egyptians shelled the rafts the IDF used for shipping over tanks, sinking several. Next, a monumental traffic jam on the roads to the canal – there must have been some six thousand vehicles including perhaps 300 fifty-ton tanks – prevented the special 'roller bridge' the Israelis had built for just such an eventuality from being towed into position. The night of 16/17 October was particularly difficult as the Egyptian 2nd Army, coming from the north, attacked the flank of the Israeli corridor leading to the canal in an attempt to close it.

Dayan spent part of this time at Southern Front Headquarters, part at those of the divisions. As news of each mishap came in – this unit had come under heavy fire and been all but annihilated, that road was still closed and could not be opened to Israeli traffic – there were decisions to be made. Whether to halt the crossing or to proceed; whether to send in more tanks or wait until the bridge had been built; whether to spread out from the bridgehead or wait until it had been reinforced first. All these were critically important matters which, unless properly handled, might cause the crossing to fail and/or the forces in 'Africa' to be cut off. Back in Tel Aviv, Ms Meir was not familiar with military affairs and did not pretend to interfere in them. Hence most of the debate took place between Dayan, Elazar (who would fly over for the purpose), Bar Lev, Bar Lev's chief of staff General Uri Ben Ari, Sharon and Adan.

All six were experienced officers, though with widely different views and temperaments. All had known each other for many years, with all the strong likes and dislikes that such acquaintance engenders. They would hold their meetings reclining on some relatively safe sand dune, addressing each other by their first names or nicknames such as 'Moshe', 'Arik', 'Dado' (Elazar), 'Bren' (Adan), etc. Underneath, however, the tension was palpable; nor were things made easier by the columns of smoke and noise of firing that could be seen and heard in the distance. As the most senior man present, Dayan could have overruled the rest. In practice, except for one decision to discontinue an attack by Sharon's division on a stronghold east of the canal, he did not do so, even when he disliked the way things were going. With Elazar and Dayan only present part of the time, the voice that counted was that of Bar Lev. As chief of staff, he had commanded both Elazar and Sharon. With the former he got along – they were both ex-PALMACHniks – but Sharon hated him. Though no military genius, he had a well-balanced personality who never lost his temper and spoke v-e-r-y s-l-o-w-l-y; another strong point was his ability to get along well with Ms Meir. Now he tended towards caution, warning Sharon in particular not to move forward too fast before the corridor leading to the crossing could be secured. Sharon, who believed in manoeuvre and who had long been famous as a risk-taker, obeyed the order only half-heartedly. As he later wrote, what he would have liked was to hit Bar Lev in the face.

In the early afternoon of 17 October Dayan and Sharon went forward to the actual crossing point. First of all, while still on the east bank of the canal, they came under intense Egyptian artillery bombardment. With shells exploding all around, they took shelter in one of the earthen 'courts' that had been prepared especially for the purpose, where they met a group of Egyptian prisoners who recognized Dayan and asked for medical assistance and food. After being carried across the 150-yard wide waterway on one of the IDF's heavy rafts, they spent some time touring the area to the west of it on foot. The fighting in this area had been bitter and it was not a pretty sight. Burnt-out blackened vehicles littered the ground and mutilated bodies were scattered about, some of the latter being gnawed at by stray dogs. In the area east of the canal, which he visited later on the same day, the slaughter had been even greater. He was not a man to let such things deter him or influence his decisions in any way, yet this time he found it hard to keep his feelings under control. Having spent the night in Tel Aviv, the next morning found him back on the west bank of the canal, where he met with Sharon and Adan and watched the fighting at close range.

By the 18th the Israeli bridgehead, which initially had been small and only held by light forces, was being rapidly expanded towards the west and south in particular. Partly because it *had* been small, partly because lower echelons did what they could to hide its significance from their superiors, the Egyptian High Command had initially not realized its significance. Now it was becoming increasingly clear that they had begun to do so; the more they realized the seriousness of the Israeli incursion, the more insistent they became in pressing their Soviet patrons into making the Security Council impose a ceasefire. Dayan, who had experienced a similar situation not in one but two previous wars, saw what was coming. The IDF was too tired and too depleted to expand the bridgehead in two directions in order to encircle both the 2nd and 3rd Egyptian Armies. A decision had to be made as to which was to be given priority; as it turned out, this was the last important decision he was called on to make before the guns fell silent. In the end it was Adan and not Sharon who received the green light as well as whatever reinforcements were available. Fighting their way south against tough opposition, Adan's men reached the city of Suez on the evening of 24 October.

As Dayan describes it in his memoirs, the war had ended well for Israel. In the north, not only had the IDF regained all its losses – as well as capturing several additional critically important observation posts on Mount Hermon – but it had occupied a piece of Syrian territory that could be used for negotiations. As in 1967 the Syrian Army had not been destroyed. However, its offensive capability, particularly the crucial armoured divisions, had been spent. Since then the effectiveness of those divisions has fluctuated. Seen from the perspective of late 2003, it seems that they were never again restored to their full power; but this was something Dayan could not have foreseen. In the south, the Bar Lev Line had fallen and the IDF had failed to dislodge the Egyptians from the strip of territory they had occupied in the western Sinai. It had, however, counterattacked, broken through, and crossed the canal. Having defeated the Egyptian anti-aircraft defences on the ground, it surrounded the smaller one of the two Egyptian armies, bringing it to the point where, but for the ceasefire, it would have been forced to surrender for lack of supplies.

Against these achievements were the losses. Arab losses in both men and material had been much heavier than those of Israel but Dayan was experienced enough to know that this would not give their leaders too many sleepness nights. Counting those who were killed after the ceasefire of 24 October as well as those who died later of their wounds, Israel mourned the loss of approximately 2,700 lives. The fighting in this war had been much harder than at any time since 1948 and the Arab troops had held their own. This was true not only during the first days of hostilities, but also in the later stages when the IDF had recovered from its shock, mobilized its reserves, and changed its tactics in order to cope with the challenge posed by anti-aircraft and, particularly, by anti-tank missiles.

As for the events leading to the war, he still felt that, in the matter of working towards an interim settlement with Egypt, Israel could have done more. Once the War of Attrition had ended and the ceasefire along the Suez Canal appeared to be stable, nobody, either in Israel or abroad, considered the question to be particularly urgent. As a result, negotiations were not pushed forward as hard as they might have been. Basically, however, the war had been a direct result of the unwillingness of Egypt and Syria to trade peace for territory lost in 1967. What they wanted was land without peace, which demand could, of course, be met only by means of a victorious campaign.

Already during the first day of the war Dayan, ever a political animal and a veteran of the Lavon 'Affair', had realized that there would be a post mortem investigation. Relying on his assistant, one Lieutenant Colonel Aryeh Braun, he took care to record everything he said and everything said to him. At his initiative, at least one important meeting was held with only Braun and those directly involved attending. The outcome was that Dayan was the one person who possessed a record of all conversations; he was also the only one who consulted professional lawyers when preparing his defence. Since he had taken pains to record everything, he was better prepared to face the subsequent investigations than his subordinates were. When the latter accused him of shirking responsibility, in reality they were jealous, resentful of the fact that he was better prepared to face the music than they. There was, however, a price to be paid. As other people followed his example in subsequent investigations, the trust on which the IDF had always been based and which constituted perhaps its strongest point began to be undermined.

In November 1973 the Commission of Investigation he had anticipated was in fact set up. Its chairman was Shimon Agranat, president of Israel's High Court; the members, Moshe Landau, a High Court justice, Yitzhak Nebentzal, the State Comptroller, General (ret.) Yigael Yadin, and General (ret.) Haim Laskov. The commission took five months to conduct its investigation and publish an interim report. Much to the chagrin of many Israelis, Dayan was exonerated. To understand this decision it is important to realize the structure of Israel's decision-making machinery as it was at the time. Unlike some other countries, Israel did not have a National Security Council with overall responsibility for advising the Prime Minister. Consequently the chief of military intelligence wore a double hat; not only did he advise the chief of staff, but he was also responsible for drawing up the *national* intelligence estimate both for the Minister of Defence and for the Prime Minister. These arrangements meant that Dayan, and behind him Ms Meir, only had access to such information as Zeira chose to submit to them; and Zeira, it turned out, had neither used the 'special' intelligence-collecting means at his disposal nor informed his superiors of his failure to do so. Therefore, the commission ruled, so long as Dayan followed what information he had, and acted on it, he had not been remiss in his duty.

The men who, in the commission's view, *had* been remiss were located further down. Besides Zeira, who became the main culprit, three other senior intelligence officers had to go. The commission's most prominent victims, however, were Elazar and Gonen. Elazar was said to be 'personally responsible for what happened on the eve of the war both in respect to the estimate of the situation and in respect to the IDF's [deficient] readiness'. Since the commission's mandate was to investigate the events up to and including 8 October only, his outstanding performance during the rest of the war was ignored. Gonen was blamed for his confused leadership during the first days of the war and, specifically, the counter-offensive of 8 October when he had failed to control and co-ordinate his subordinates. Of the three, Zeira turned to business and later published a book in which he blamed the commission for its lack of objectivity and even hinted that Laskov had been indebted to Dayan for giving him the job of Military Ombudsman at a time when he had nothing else to do. Elazar died soon afterwards of a heart attack, and the task of writing his apology was left to a well-known Israeli novelist. The strangest fate overtook Gonen. In 1967 he had been admired, nay worshipped, for leading the armoured brigade that had broken through near Rafah. Now he was presented as a martinet, which he was, and as a brutal and stupid man, which he was not. He was ostracized and left the country, going to the Central African Republic in search of diamonds. After his death, he became the 'hero' of a play in which he was inflated into some kind of inhuman monster.

In absolving Dayan the commission did not look into his parliamentary responsibility, arguing that this was a political question and, as such, beyond its competence. Dayan himself was well aware of the problem; in fact, as discussed above, one of his first moves after the war had been to go to Ms Meir and renew his offer to resign if she no longer had confidence in him. She was a tough and outspoken politician whose attitude to Dayan had been shaped at the time when he and Shimon Peres, 'bright young men' (her own expression),[99] had tried to outflank her and the rest of the party veterans. He in turn liked to tell how, at one of his meetings with King Abdullah of Jordan, the latter, learning that Golda Meir had been appointed Israeli ambassador to Moscow, advised the government to leave her there. As so often, she did the right thing. She would not fire her Minister of Defence so long as negotiations towards Separation of Forces Agreements with Egypt and Syria were going on, Israeli prisoners were in Arab hands, many reservists remained with the colours and a fresh outbreak of hostilities remained possible. Instead, at this stage, it was Dayan's chief critic in the government who had to go. He was Moshe Haim Shapira, the man who, six years earlier, had brought Dayan into the government.

If the commission absolved Dayan and Ms Meir resolved to keep him for the time being, public opinion could not be as easily placated. Like the army – which formed part of it and of which it was so inordinately proud – the Israeli people had been overconfident and contemptuous of their Arab enemies, even to the point of inventing derogatory names for them (which Dayan never did). Like that army, they were taken by surprise when hostilities broke out and emerged from the war in something of a daze. Those who feel powerless will look for a scapegoat. In 1967 Dayan had to some extent reaped where Eshkol, Rabin, and the General Staff had sown. Now no-one, not even Ms Meir, was more suited to the new role than the one-eyed soldier who, for so many years past, had stood as the very symbol of Israeli military power. Abetted by his rivals in the government, the same media which had hung on his every word now attacked him mercilessly. People could not forgive him for their own shortcomings; he was accused of hedonism, negligence, insensitivity, arrogance, overconfidence in face of the enemy, unwillingness to take responsibility and, early in the war, black pessimism bordering on panic. Even harder, emotionally speaking, were demonstrations in which people – including some he knew – called him a 'murderer'. Pitiless towards himself, his character had long contained more than a hint of contempt for his fellow men. This feeling was now strengthened.

In April, the time for reckoning came. The elections of December 1973 had given MAPAI and its allies a solid majority in Parliament, the last time this was to happen. Now that the Separation of Forces Agreements with both Egypt and Syria had been signed, Ms Meir, now 75 years old, had reached the end of the line. Her successor was Yitzhak Rabin. Twenty-two years younger than she, he had only just returned from Washington, DC, where, in Israeli eyes at any rate, he had covered himself with glory; thus his greatest asset was that he was uninvolved in the war that had just ended. He brought with him Peres as Minister of Defence and Allon as Foreign Minister. Both because of Dayan's complicated relationship with the former chief of staff and because of his role in recent events, it was obvious that there would be no place in the new government for him. Besides, his self-confidence was at an all-time low. Whether he admitted it or not, he needed a break; he resigned his post as Minister of Defence and went home to Zahala. He was lonelier than ever, and had he still not managed to find domestic peace there is no knowing what might have followed. Fortunately for him, he had Rahel to share both happiness and sorrow.

CHAPTER 7

Fall and Rise

Dayan spent the first year or so after his resignation writing his memoirs. Assisted by two of his veteran secretaries, he went through mountains of documents that had accumulated over the years. In an army famous for its lackadaisical methods he had always been notorious for recording everything he did or said; looking back, perhaps it was he who was famous and the methods notorious. During the first few weeks he was hesitant, not trusting in his own skill as a writer and asking Yael for advice. Soon, however, he took the bit between his teeth and wrote and wrote. Work was therapy; by the time the memoirs were published he had recovered his self-confidence. The product, while not actually a masterpiece, is a very finely crafted piece of work. Not only does it offer keen insight into the man but, as one reviewer wrote, it also provides a panoramic history of the country in which he lived and the trials it went through.

As so often with Dayan, however, what he did not say was as important as what he did. For example, both his role in the 'Season' and his activities as an 'adviser for Arab affairs' are mentioned only in bare outline. It remains unclear why he first prohibited the IDF from approaching the Suez Canal – at one point he even threatened to court-martial General Gavish – and then dropped his demand. He does not explain whether, in the winter of 1968–69, he was in favour of building the Bar Lev Line or opposed to it. Nor does he explain why he at first objected to the appointment of Elazar as chief of staff and then dropped his objections. Most important of all, he does not say anything about the controversy that broke out between Generals Bar Lev and Sharon as to whether a more aggressive conduct of operations on Israel's part might have brought the 1973 War to an earlier and more successful end. One interpretation of these omissions is that, on these and other questions, he was overruled; another, that he was responsible for them or at least concurred with them but did not want to take responsibility. What we do learn about are his love of farming, archaeology and Rahel, feelings made all the more impressive by the occasional touch of humour and the poetic yet simple language in which they are voiced. Another strong point of the book is that it does not openly criticize anybody. If there were people to whom he took an intense dislike, he kept that fact to himself.

Like Dayan, Israel had come out of the war bruised and embattled. Like him, it needed time to pull itself together, and it fell to Rabin and his cabinet to take the first decisive steps in that direction. The dead had to be buried, the wounded healed or, if that was impossible, given the care that they needed. Economically speaking, the eighteen-day war had cost the country the equivalent of an entire year's national product. Living standards, which with one short interruption had been steadily rising for over a decade and a half, suddenly plummeted. Compared to the period before 1973, American financial aid was increased seven-fold. Combined with rising oil prices the result was a sharp increase in inflation, which in 1974 alone, reached 60 per cent.

From a defence point of view, the most important long-term problem was to prepare the IDF for another possible war against the Arab countries. The most immediate problems were in the north, where Lebanon had turned into a hotbed of terrorism and was sliding towards civil war. By contrast, and in spite of some tense moments, the borders with Syria and Jordan remained almost completely quiet. In September 1975 Rabin concluded a Second Separation of Forces Agreement with Egypt that resulted in the return of a large slice of the Sinai. As part of the deal, which had been arranged with American assistance, the IDF's stores were filled to bursting with new weaponry. Compared to the period before 1973, the air force was expanded by another 50 per cent and the number of divisions doubled. The new hardware was more advanced than the old; thus the force which, at the beginning of Dayan's career, had been armed with nothing more than bolt-action rifles, was catapulted into the era of high-technology. Israel's arms industry also grew until, at peak, it employed one quarter of the industrial workforce. In fact, the entire country was being turned into a vast arsenal.

Dayan's part in all this was marginal. Though he was still a Member of Parliament, his duties bored him and only took up a small part of his time, some of the rest being taken up by archaeology. Soon, having finished his autobiography and discovered how much money there was to be made from writing, he launched another project called *Living with the Bible*. In some ways it was his finest work. In it he draws parallels between the history of modern Zionism, including his own, and that of the ancient heroes; for example, he compares his own assault on the French police station in 1941 with the stealthy attack that Jonathan, son of King Saul, made on the Philistines thousands of years earlier. Thus he woos his country, its often harsh but beautiful vistas, its unique climatic characteristics – many of which are known by Arabic names – and the people who have lived in it and shed their blood over it.

Politically speaking, his main concern seems to have been with the intense quantitative arms race on which Israel was now engaged. This was a time when the energy crisis was causing the Arab states to be flushed with petrodollars as never before (or since) in their history. To Dayan, it appeared as if such a race might push Israel to the breaking point and beyond. Though part of the bill was paid with American money, the economic burden was intolerable. What is more, finding enough people of suitable quality to act as officers and pilots was becoming very difficult; in the rush to expand, the ground forces in particular suffered. As long ago as 1955–57, Dayan had been among those who advocated developing a nuclear deterrent. Now, confirming what foreign sources had been saying for years, he suggested that Israel raise its nuclear profile; and was sharply attacked by the media with Rabin at their head each time he did so. Rabin, after all, had Israel's relations with the USA to think of. Yet it would not be surprising to learn that Dayan did this after co-ordinating with the Prime Minister and, above all, his good friend and the architect of Israel's nuclear programme, Peres. In doing so, their objective may have been to deter the Arab states, especially Syria, from launching another war against Israel; also, to press the USA into increasing its military aid.

In May 1977, elections were held and the thirty-year rule of MAPAI – now known as Labour – ended. The victors were Menahem Begin and his right-wing Likud Party. The second man in the new government was Weizman who had run the campaign and, as his reward, was appointed Minister of Defence. From June 1967 to August 1970 Begin had been Minister without Portfolio in a national unity cabinet. Hearing Ms Meir pronounce the word 'withdrawal', he had reacted by rising from his seat, crossing the floor of Parliament, and taking his place with the opposition. In 1974–75 he and his party had criticized both Meir and Rabin for their alleged weakness, opposing the Separation of Forces Agreements and taking a hawkish position in foreign affairs generally. Though Begin did not often mention the Sinai, he was committed to retaining the Golan Heights. Above all else, he was determined to prevent the partition of what he called 'the historic Land of Israel'. In other words, to ensure that Israel retained full control over the West Bank and, of course, East Jerusalem.

Re-elected as a representative for Labour, Dayan was now a member of the opposition. His relationship with Begin went back to 1944 when, as part of his role in the 'Season', Dayan had at least one long conversation with him. Unlike Ben Gurion, whose hatred for Begin was such that he refused to call him by his name, and unlike Rabin, who at one point during the election campaign had called Begin 'an archaeological exhibit', Dayan had no quarrel with the man. Unlike some, he recognized the right-wingers for their patriotism and willingness to make sacrifices. Conversely, Begin admired Dayan. In 1967, he did what he could to have him appointed Minister of Defence in the National Coalition Government. During the 1973 War, when he was once again serving as head of the opposition, he had met Dayan and suggested that the IDF occupy Damascus to rescue the Jews who lived there. Since doing so would require vast numbers of troops that Israel did not have, the idea demonstrated an astonishing ignorance of military affairs, one which was later to cost Israel dear.

Even before the electoral victory Begin, speaking in strict confidence, told some of his closest associates that if he were to form a government he would ask Dayan to act as Foreign Minister. Ideologue though he was, Begin well understood that his image was that of a fire-eating ex-terrorist. Dayan would help him redress the balance by presenting a more reasonable face to the world, and to both the Arabs and the United States as Israel's only ally; besides, the result would be to split the opposition. Hardly were the elections over than he did in fact offer the post to Dayan. Amidst howls of protest from the members of his own party, Dayan accepted; to him, it was a heaven-sent opportunity to repair his tarnished reputation. Before entering the government he spoke to Begin and ascertained that the new government would not proclaim Israeli sovereignty over any part of the Occupied Territories as long as peace negotiations were going on. The deal was struck and the promise kept. It was only after Dayan left the cabinet that Begin passed a vote through Parliament formally annexing the Golan Heights.

By this time little of Dayan's old popularity remained, and the members of his own party regarded him as a traitor. He was a Labourite surrounded by members of Likud, many of whom had not yet forgotten his role in the 'Season'. Having crossed from one party to another, he had even less organized support than before. His sole assets were his international reputation and his supposed ability to get along with the Arabs; and even that was a reason for some to regard him with suspicion. Nor was his relationship with Begin always easy. Not only did the Prime Minister pull all the strings – replicating the situation as it had been under Ms Meir, when it was always Dayan who proposed, Begin who disposed – but he was an orator who was fascinated by the sound of his own voice. At the slightest provocation he would launch into bombastic speeches about Israel's sacred patrimony, the persecution of the Jews, historical justice, and so on and so forth. All this may have endeared him to those who voted for him, but in conducting diplomatic negotiations it constituted an obstacle; worse still, it had the effect of arraying the Americans with the Egyptians against Israel. Dayan, in whose eyes bombast was associated with his father and other Zionist rhetoricians, realized this. As the Prime Minister rattled away the Foreign Minister would often be seen holding his head in his hands. Later, to let off steam, he would go for a solitary walk.

As always, he entered office determined to ignore all aspects of his job except those which interested him and which he considered most essential. For several years he had been convinced that Egypt was prepared to move in the direction of peace. In 1974, still at his post as Minister of Defence, he had said as much at a pilots' graduation ceremony; coming so soon after the 1973 War, it was a daring and far-sighted statement. Now it was time to see if his beliefs could be translated into something practical. As it later turned out – this was by no means evident from the outset – the times were propitious. On the Israeli home front Begin and his colleagues were in a position to do what they themselves had prevented their predecessors from doing, i.e. move towards peace without giving rise to shrieks of dismay – and parliamentary votes of no confidence – from the opposition. In Egypt, the population was becoming tired of President Sadat's claims that they had won the 1973 War and wanted something more concrete to show for their 'victory'. On the one hand, launching another offensive against Israel was extremely dangerous; if foreign sources could be believed, it might even meet with a nuclear response. On the other, Egypt was in great economic difficulty and bread-riots had broken out. To solve his problems Sadat desperately needed some success in foreign policy, the more so because, if he succeeded, he might perhaps be able to attract American economic aid.

Dayan spent the first few days in office preparing a detailed memorandum for Begin. In it, he outlined his views concerning the position Israel should take in case multilateral peace talks with the Arab countries in Geneva, presided over by the USA and USSR, should resume after having been abandoned three years previously. The issues remaining from over twenty years of warfare were numerous and complex. They included, besides the question of borders with three different Arab countries, the establishment of arrangements that would guarantee Israel's security; the distribution of water (in the case of Syria); the future of the Palestinians (both those in the West Bank and in the Gaza Strip); eventual links between the Palestinians and the neighbouring Arab states that might assume responsibility for them; the status of the Palestinian refugees both inside and outside the Occupied Territories; the question of Jerusalem; and so on. His conclusion was that it would be impossible to solve all problems at once. Instead, it would be necessary to proceed step by step. Over some of the issues it might be possible to conclude interim agreements rather than proceed directly to final ones.

Had it depended on him, he would have started with Hussein of Jordan. Like many Israelis, he had a sneaking liking for 'Hussi' or 'the Little King', as he was affectionately known. He had dealt with him before. In 1973 Hussein had warned Ms Meir personally against the impending Egyptian–Syrian attack; and when Dayan left his post as Minister of Defence, he had received a courteous farewell letter from Israel's royal neighbour. Now, in meeting him again and offering him important parts of the West Bank, Dayan was merely following precedents set by Allon – as Ms Meir's deputy – before 1973, and by Rabin – as Prime Minister – after that. As he had done in all previous meetings, however, Hussein refused to play along. As an Arab leader, he said, he neither could nor would 'propose to a single Arab to leave his brethren and join Israel';[100] the Israelis compared him to a small child that stamped its foot and pouted. In any case, Begin would never have agreed to an arrangement that might have entrusted any part of the West Bank to a non-Israeli government, the prevention of which was, after all, what his entire policy and even world-view were all about.

Both before and after 1973 Syria had been the most intractable of Israel's enemies, refusing even to come to the Geneva Conference. In the event, this worked in Israel's favour. As the French proverb has it, those who absent themselves are always wrong. Since Damascus refused to do anything for itself, everyone else could ignore it as well; here, at any rate, was something on which Israel and Egypt saw eye to eye. In making the first approaches, Israel was fortunate in that it could count on help from the King of Morocco, Hassan II, who was prepared to act as a go-between. Using another intermediary, President Ceaucescu of Romania, Begin had already passed a message to Sadat that he wanted a meeting. There was also some movement on the other side. When Sadat paid his first visit to the newly installed President Carter, he was told that the best thing he could do to further peace was to meet with Begin.

Disguised with sunglasses and a false moustache, Dayan made two trips to Morocco. On the first he spoke to the king, asking him to mediate. On the second he met Egypt's Deputy Prime Minister and Sadat's special envoy, Hassan Tuami. Like Dayan, Tuami had an intelligence background that included various hatchet jobs and involved operating in the grey area between the military and politics. Unlike Dayan, who was a world-famous figure, Tuami usually operated far from the limelight. He also differed from most members of the Egyptian elite in that he was a devout Muslim. To prove it, he had divorced his first wife – a former beauty queen of Finland – and wore a beard; last but not least, in the endless series of Arab–Israeli Wars he had lost both a brother and a brother-in-law. Dayan was undoubtedly the right Israeli to talk to him. After all, some of his own countrymen regarded him as more Arab than Jewish.

With Hassan present for some of the time, the two men circled each other like dogs for more than seven hours, each trying to take the measure of the other. For decades, the only Arab head of state who had agreed to meet with his Israeli counterparts had been King Hussein. Even these meetings had to take place in secret. Both Israelis and Jordanians well remembered how King Abdullah had been assassinated for his alleged collaboration with Israel; at the time, indeed, Hussein himself had been standing right beside his grandfather. Initially Tuami demanded that the meeting between Sadat and Begin take place only *after* all the territories that Israel had occupied were handed back. By contrast, Dayan's task was to convince his interlocutor that the order should be reversed. Begin, he hinted, was sufficiently prepared to grant concessions in order to make it worth while for the Egyptian President to take the risk; to enable direct negotiations to take place, both the Geneva Conference and American mediation should be dispensed with for the time being. Though Dayan was careful to avoid any specific commitments, the talks were far more detailed than anything previously attempted. He must have plucked the right strings. A few weeks later, Sadat stunned his own Parliament by proclaiming his readiness to go 'to the end of the world and even to the *Knesset* in Jerusalem' if that could push the cause of peace forward. He did so, what is more, without co-ordinating with the Americans first.

Although he had played a crucial role in laying down the groundwork, to Dayan as to most Israelis Sadat's decision to go to Jerusalem came as a surprise. For decades, whenever an Israeli baby was born its parents would offer a silent prayer that, when he or she turned 18, he or she would not have to serve in the army; Yael says her father had expressed the same feeling with regard to his own grandchildren. Now he wrote a short poem in honour of the event, which was preserved by his then office manager, Elyakim Rubinstein:

> A great wind has come out of nowhere
> Out of the sky, the bells of peace rang.
> President Sadat landed in Israel –
> Was it real, or did we dream?

Wherever Sadat went he was given a rousing welcome by the Israeli people. Still, during the visit no detailed negotiations took place and no agreement was reached. Instead the Egyptian President, speaking in Israel's Parliament, reiterated his demand that, in return for 'no more war', Israel withdraw not just from Egyptian territory but from all the rest as well. He specifically included East Jerusalem; in addition, he wanted recognition for what he called 'the legitimate rights of the Palestinian people'.

In December Dayan, this time accompanied by Rubinstein, met with Tuami for the third time. He was beginning to realize that, in dealing with Egypt, Israel was facing two separate problems – and that it was the relationship between them that was critical. The first was bilateral: in other words, the price Israel would be obliged to pay in return for an Egyptian promise to end three decades of belligerency, sign a peace treaty, establish normal relations between the two states and live peacefully ever after. The second, and perhaps more difficult, was the need to avoid the impression that, by entering into a separate treaty with Israel, Egypt with Sadat at its head was simply leaving the Palestinians to their fate. Such a treaty would mean breaking ranks with the rest of the Arab world and, as many of the latter's members would and did say, betraying it. The long-term domestic consequences were also incalculable.

Over the next fourteen months – the Camp David Agreements were only signed on 26 March 1979 – the negotiations took place now in Egypt, now in Israel, now in Washington, DC, and now elsewhere. No more was it necessary to hold the meetings in secret. On the contrary, each one attracted a crowd of journalists. Like vultures they swooped down on the smallest piece of information, often inventing whatever they were unable to get from the personalities involved. Initially the Israelis, Dayan included, had operated in the hope that Egypt would settle for something less than the complete evacuation of the entire Sinai. At one point or another they had wanted to retain control of the Straits of Tyran with, perhaps, a narrow strip of territory leading to it. They also tried to keep the two modern military airfields they had recently built for themselves not far from the former border; arrange for joint military patrols in the peninsula; and maintain several small Jewish settlements. The latter dated back to Dayan's own initiative as Minister of Defence, having been established south of the Gaza Strip in order to separate it from the rest of the Sinai.

One by one, Dayan was compelled to recognize that these objectives were unattainable. As Sadat himself told him in one of their rare meetings, for the Egyptian people a complete restoration of their sovereignty over the entire peninsula was axiomatic; and indeed one may venture the guess that, had he agreed to anything short of that, his regime would not have survived. At the same time, and if only to avoid friction in the future, Sadat also rejected all proposals that a number of Israelis, whether soldiers or civilians, stay in the Sinai under Egyptian sovereignty. In the end, he only made three concessions. The first, and most important by far, was his agreement to make full peace immediately after the treaty was signed. The second was to relinquish any role for Egypt in the Gaza Strip where it had ruled from 1948 to 1967 and where, the Israelis argued, a renewed presence on its part could only lead to difficulties. The third was to agree to the demilitarization of the Sinai east of the crucial passes that lead into it from Egypt proper. Separated from the nearest Egyptian troops by about a hundred miles of open desert, Israel would arguably be more secure against attack than it had been at the time the two sides had faced each other with only the Suez Canal to separate them. The campaigns of 1956 and 1967 had shown that, militarily speaking, for the Egyptians to deploy strong forces on Israel's borders, far from their own centre of power, was about the worst error they could commit. Dayan, who had been in charge on both occasions, understood this at least as well as anyone. So did his colleague, Weizman; after all, as commander of the air force he had been largely responsible for hatching the plans whereby those very forces had been hacked to pieces.

To help the Egyptians in their difficulty with the rest of the Arab world, Dayan became the first Israeli to suggest that it would be necessary to ask for American mediation. It was one of the typical volte-faces with which he never ceased to surprise his colleagues; and which, depending on the outcome, gave him a reputation now for brilliance, now for instability. When the Treaty was finally signed it was American, not Israeli military personnel who were sent to man the early-warning stations established in the Sinai to ensure that the peninsula did, in fact, remain demilitarized. It was American engineers, paid for by American money, who built two new airfields for the Israelis in the Negev to take the place of those left behind in the Sinai. Since Israel would be giving up oilfields in the Sinai, and since this was at the height of the energy crisis, it was vital for Israel to receive American guarantees of oil supplies should these become unavailable elsewhere. Finally, American economic assistance to Israel was stepped up; to help Sadat in his domestic difficulties, Egypt, too, received aid, and continues to do so to the present day. To some extent the USA stood in for Egypt, promising Begin some of the things Sadat could not or would not give in order to coax him into a deal. Thus peace in the Middle East was bought, albeit at for huge sums of money; and, equally important, with the certainty that the USA would remain involved for many years to come.

Achieving all this was anything but easy. *Detente* had ended, and the so-called Second Cold War was in full swing. To many observers it seemed as if the USSR, with Leonid Brezhnev at its head, was going from strength to strength; shaken by Western debacles in Angola, Ethiopia and Iran, President Carter was as eager for a foreign-policy triumph as President Sadat was to repossess the Sinai. Against that background, he sometimes tended to lean too much on Israel. According to William Quandt, then a member of the US National Security Council and later the author of the most important book on the Israeli–Egyptian peace process, by enlisting the USA in trilateral talks Dayan had 'played a weak hand with consummate political skill'.[101] Now it was his job to make the Americans tone down their expectations of Israel. He used his old and trusted methods: once, when the American Ambassador to Tel Aviv, Samuel Lewis, had just handed him a particularly imperious message from the State Department, Dayan asked whether he would also point out the place for Israel to sign. In this way he protected Begin from the Americans;

without his intervention such high-handedness might well have forced the Prime Minister to call off the talks. Whether anybody else could have achieved this is doubtful.

Although there were differences inside the Israeli camp, when it came to the need to reach an agreement with Egypt all three key figures – Begin, Dayan, and Weizman – acted in concert. In the event, it was Weizman who took the lead. Both he and Dayan were famous experts on military affairs, completely outclassing Begin, whose knowledge of the subject had been acquired during his youth in Poland and had barely developed since. As long as his principal advisers agreed that this or that asset could be given away without undue risk, there was little chance that the Prime Minister would refuse to comply; the time when, sustained by mood-lifting drugs, he considered himself infallible was still in the future. With respect to the Palestinian question, where ideological considerations played a much more important role, the situation was different. Here it was Dayan's special mission to persuade not only the Egyptians but, at least as difficult, his own superior. Begin had come to power by promising not to let any part of 'Judea and Samaria', as he called them, slip from Israel's grasp. In keeping this promise he had both Parliament and people solidly behind him.

As we have seen, Sadat could not ignore the Palestinian question without being considered a traitor to the Arab people as a whole. As we have also seen, Dayan himself had long been unhappy with the situation in the Occupied Territories and sought some means whereby it might be resolved. For him, as for most Israelis at the time, there could be no question of negotiating with the Palestinian Liberation Organization (PLO), whose official objective was to return the refugees to their home and set up a single 'secular and democratic' state reaching from the Mediterranean to the River Jordan. Israelis interpreted this meaning the destruction of their own state, as well they might. Besides, the PLO was a terrorist organization; and talking with terrorists was considered taboo both for practical reasons – fear lest giving way to one act of terror would merely lead to another one – and emotional ones. The efforts of Dayan and others to enlist Hussein to help them out of the impasse had not been fruitful, given that the king always took a position of all or nothing. Finally, and if only because the PLO threatened to assassinate anybody who did try to settle with Israel, attempts to negotiate with Palestinian leaders inside the territories also led nowhere.

The situation called for ingenuity, and ingenuity was something of which Dayan had plenty; turning the Biblical phrase on its head, he used to say that 'by stratagems is peace made'. His own objective, in the West Bank in particular, was to ensure that the watershed remained in Israeli hands, given that this was the only way to defend against an attack from the east. To achieve this, he thought, more was needed than just military bases and installations; what was needed were solid 'fists' of Jewish settlements that would surround them and make it that much harder to remove them by political means. The population, he believed, should be permitted to lead its own life, and the less the Israelis interfered, the better. The two considerations together led to the 'autonomy' plan; in a way, it was a logical development of the ideas he had been playing with from 1967 on. Israel would neither give up control of the territories to others nor renounce the right of its people to buy land and settle there if they wished. It would, however, do away with the military government Dayan himself had established in the aftermath of the 1967 War. Instead, an eleven-member Council would be established, elected by a popular vote, controlling most aspects of life except defence. As Dayan himself told President Carter, Israel alone would decide which armed force should cross the Jordan from east to west.

Such was Dayan's own plan, the fruit of deeply held beliefs concerning Israeli defence requirements on the one hand and the best way to deal with the Palestinians on the other. Now his task was to sell the idea to Begin and Sadat; with Begin, he also had to avoid the impression that Israel would be giving in to the American demands that it concede too much, too quickly. In some ways he was the right man for the job. In others, his task was not made easier by his personality and the reputation that followed from it. Many in the Arab world saw 'Mussa' Dayan as clever and resourceful; the kind of person who might strip you of your socks without first taking off your shoes. Consequently Sadat preferred not to talk to him in person, leaving that task to his underlings. Instead he spoke to 'Ezra' – as he called him – Weizman, perhaps identifying him as the weak link in Israel's leading trio. At the same time, and as the Americans noted, the more advanced the negotiations, the less Dayan enjoyed the confidence of Begin. With his dark-rimmed glasses, old-fashioned manners and heavily accentuated English, the Prime Minister won few friends for himself or for Israel. He suspected his Foreign Minister of being prepared to give away more than he himself was, yet it was he who had to bear the ultimate responsibility. Accordingly he tried to do everything in person, even to the point where, drawing on his original training as a lawyer, he himself drew up legal documents.

In the end Dayan's efforts, supported by those of President Carter and US Secretary of State Cyrus Vance, were successful, but only up to a point: the real issue had not been tackled, thus laying the basis for future difficulties that remain unresolved to the present day. Begin agreed to 'start negotiations [over the fate of the West Bank and the Gaza Strip] within a month from the exchange of the instruments of ratification of the Peace Treaty'; also, to aim at 'establishing [an] elected self-governing authority' that would permit 'the Israeli military government and its civilian administration [to be] withdrawn'[102] over a transitional period of five years. By postponing the question of sovereignty Begin's aim was to ensure that Israel retained control. To Sadat, the aim of the exercise was precisely the opposite, i.e. to leave the way open towards a eventual Israeli withdrawal from all the Occupied Territories. At the time, Dayan's own position on this question was probably closer to Begin's than to Sadat's. Already during his meetings with Tuami he had told Sadat that there would never be a Palestinian state. However, it is conceivable that, had the Palestinian autonomy proved to be successful, he might have taken a more flexible position.

It remained to ensure that, should the status of the territories not be resolved within five years as was expected, the peace between Israel and Egypt would still remain undisturbed. This was the famous question known as 'linkage'; in the end, the importance of the 'linkage' was precisely that it did *not* exist. To achieve this, the Peace Treaty was drawn up on a strictly bilateral basis and did not contain a single word about the Palestinian question or, indeed, any other Arab–Israeli one. However, it was accompanied by several appendices and letters. Some of these dealt with the promises that the US had made to Israel. The most important one was a joint letter from Begin and Sadat to Carter in which the plan for the West Bank and Gaza was outlined. Legally speaking, the treaty stood on its own like some Rock of Gibraltar. Politically, of course, all sides well understood (or should have) that a link did exist and that future developments in the Middle East would depend at least partly on progress towards solving the Palestinian question.

Israel's withdrawal from the Sinai, which was scheduled to last three years, proceeded almost without a hitch. In accordance with the treaty, diplomatic relations were established and Egypt undertook to provide Israel with oil. The one significant problem concerned a small piece of territory south of Elath. Using old maps, the Israelis insisted that it belonged to them, and they evacuated it only after an International Court was convened and ruled against them. By the time this happened, Dayan was dead. As anticipated, differences arose over the question of the Palestinian territories that still remained under Israeli occupation. These did not, however, overturn the Peace Treaty with Egypt which, on both sides, had been drafted with just this possibility in mind; but they did cause the atmosphere to deteriorate. This became much more pronounced after Sadat was assassinated in October 1981 and his place taken by Hosni Mubarak. In fact, the negotiations that were held over the establishment of an 'elected self-governing [Palestinian] authority' stalled from the beginning. Meanwhile Sharon, acting as Begin's Minister of Agriculture, orchestrated a massive effort to settle the territories with as many Jews as possible.

Dayan's role in all of this was once again marginal. Begin had always been something of a manic-depressive. Now that the treaty with Egypt had been signed his self-confidence skyrocketed; with Sharon at his side, in little more than three years he was to launch his country into the misguided Lebanese adventure that left approximately 1,500 dead for no appreciable gain. By contrast, Dayan's own usefulness to the Prime Minister declined, as did his influence in the cabinet. To many of his right-wing colleagues Dayan appeared a dangerous man. He did not share their semi-mystical ideology and he was prepared to give away assets that they were determined to retain. In the cabinet he voted against the ongoing massive requisitioning of Palestinian land. His colleagues retaliated by refusing to let him lead the Israeli delegation to the autonomy talks. He was also sick, having been diagnosed with cancer of the colon, for which he was operated on in May 1979, just two months after the Camp David Agreements. He had always been very strong and, had he been asked whether the disease might have anything to do with his state of mind, he would no doubt have said that that the idea constituted 'twopenny psychology'. For decades he had struggled with pain, but by this time he was worn out. In his book about the peace process he writes of how he had recurrent dreams of crawling into an underground passage and lying down comfortably in his grave, overlooking the valley of his birth. Death, which had never held any terror for him, was beginning to look positively attractive.

Twelve years had passed since the 1967 victory in which Dayan himself had played such a large part. Partly because of his own liberal policies in minimizing friction with the population, the Occupied Territories were still surprisingly quiet; indeed one could go almost anywhere, unarmed, without feeling in danger. Nevertheless, whatever else he may have had in mind, it was clear to him that direct Israeli rule over almost 2 million Palestinians was untenable in the long run. One way or another 'the blemish of conquest',[103] as he later put it, would have to be removed: even if it meant having to negotiate over that sacred cow, the future of Jerusalem; even if it had to be done without an agreement; and even if it meant that Israel had to take unilateral action. Nor, unlike many other Israelis, was Dayan blind to the human aspect of the situation. Whatever else, to him Arabs had always been flesh and blood just like himself. He neither looked down on them as 'primitive' nor considered them particularly wicked. Almost to his last day he continued to talk to them and, as he liked best, haggle with them over antiques that they had found and he wanted to buy. When Begin's government at one point prohibited the opening of a bank in Gaza because it had the word 'Palestinian' in its name, he thought Israel had gone 'bonkers'.[104]

His remaining duties as Foreign Minister did not particularly interest him, nor had he ever cared for office for its own reward. With Rahel in tow he paid visits to this country and that, discussed various issues with his hosts, participated in dinner parties and bought antiques. However, he felt that Israel was skirting the main problem and his heart was no longer in it. On 2 October 1979 he wrote to Begin:[105]

Last week, in a hurried conversation, I expressed to you my reservations with regard to the way the negotiations in respect to autonomy are proceeding. I told you that, under present circumstances, I do not see any point to my continued participation in the cabinet as Foreign Minister...

Though only four months have passed since the start of the negotiations, I am sorry to say they are just a pretence. Whether or not I am right in this, my view on this matter prevents me from participating in them, and I have no doubt that under such circumstances the Foreign Minister cannot perform his office...

Yours in deep friendship and esteem
Moshe Dayan

In his time he had watched some of Israel's most important leaders – Haim Weizman (Israel's first president), David Ben Gurion, Golda Meir and, in 1977, Yitzhak Rabin – holding on to the trappings of office by the skins of their teeth until they were finally forced to relinquish them. As long ago as 1957, when he was at the peak of his glory as chief of staff, he had decided that nothing of the kind would happen to him and that he would rather leave a post before he was pushed out of it against his will. Twice previously he had resigned, only to be brought back into office as much by historical events as by his own efforts. Now, at 64, he only had two years left to live.

CHAPTER 8

Looking Backward

On 25 August 2001 two Palestinian fighters penetrated an Israeli strong-hold not far from Rafah, killing two Israeli soldiers and wounding seven, before being killed themselves. A Commission of Investigation was established to look into the incident, and on 16 September its findings were published. First, it turned out that the soldiers guarding the stronghold had not given timely warning to their comrades inside, who were fast asleep. Next, the responsible company commanders responded too slowly. Next, brigade headquarters did not function properly. Perhaps the most shocking conclusions referred to the troops directly involved. Not only had they displayed very low fighting spirit, but one of them explicitly said he would not risk his life for his comrades.

On the next day, as it happened, something known as the IDF's new 'ethical code' went into force. Written by a mixed committee of army officers and university professors, it stressed such high qualities as professionalism, honesty, reliability and teamwork. Had Dayan still been around to see it, he would no doubt have expressed his contempt by crumpling it up and tossing it into the wastebasket, where it belonged. He had always known, not just with his head but with his heart, that to win one has to fight. To fight one has to be prepared to die if necessary; at one point he had ordered that no unit give up its mission before having suffered at least 50 per cent casualties. Being so courageous himself and able to inspire courage in others, he would have regarded the new code as just the kind of bombast he hated most. What is more, he would have seen it as additional proof that the qualities it called for were absent; brave men do not hunker in bunkers or send fighter-bombers to storm empty houses.

His last years were not good. Although his doctors assured him that his cancer had been cured, his heart was beginning to give way. He lost weight, which made his clothes seem to hang about his body. His complexion became sallow; his remaining eye gave him trouble, his voice had been damaged by the tube thrust into his throat while he was being operated on and he had lost most of his hair. Though he stuck to the principle of not criticizing anybody in public, the book he wrote about his role in the achievement of peace between Israel and Egypt lacks the sparkle of some of his previous works. At one point he acted as editor in chief to a daily newspaper that targeted the lowest denominator, but failed to attract many readers. He lent his name to a party that demanded the establishment of autonomy in the Occupied Territories – by unilateral action, if necessary – but failed to attract many voters. What he would have liked best was to act as a special envoy in talks with the Palestinians. Precisely because he was considered too conciliatory, though, he stood no chance of getting the appointment. Instead it went to a veteran politician, Dr Joseph Burg, who made sure there would be no progress.

In between he continued to do what he enjoyed most, i.e. to acquire antiques, clean and restore them. Some of the pieces he added during this period were magnificent and would have honoured any museum. However, his tastes were changing. In the field of archaeology as well as poetry, he had always shied away from ornamentation. More and more, he was feeling attracted to the oldest, simplest artefacts made with the crudest tools. Some were mere stones bearing a man-made scratch or two that he thought some ancient sculptor had been trying to work into the shape of various animals. Towards the end he reached the point where it no longer mattered to him whether the shapes he saw were 'really there' or merely the product of his own imagination. They were what they were, and he spent hours gazing at them.

Though his image was shaken by the 1973 War, Dayan's place in history as a highly original and inspiring commander will remain undisputed. Twice he led his country's forces – themselves, at one time, considered among the most effective ever created – into smashing victories. Few campaigns provide more convincing demonstrations of careful planning, improvisation, guile, surprise and sheer fighting power, as well as an uncommon understanding of the relationship between war and politics. Having planned and executed the one and directed the other, with his one eye he towers over them like Nelson over the Battle of Trafalgar. Not all the (fairly numerous) attempts at revisionism will wash away the glory of the dead; if Israel survives a thousand years, these will be among its finest hours. Though he did not bear ultimate responsibility, his role in the peace process, when his unique flexibility and creativity enabled him to act as a kind of lubricant between the various parties, also deserves to be remembered. To use another simile, he was like a squash ball bouncing off various walls, now slowly, now fast; never giving up, and always looking for another solution for whatever impasse presented itself.

In particular, whatever agreement has been achieved concerning the Palestinian problem is due largely to Dayan. It was a problem about which he had thought long, carefully, and not without emotional involvement. For as long as he could remember, he had been torn between his love of the Bible on the one hand and his sympathy for things Arab on the other. His policies in the Occupied Territories were originally designed to evade the question of ultimate ownership by permitting normal life to proceed. In the event, these policies were so successful for so long that it surprised even him. It was largely due to them that the Palestinian uprising was postponed by twenty years; had it broken out a decade earlier, neither Sadat's visit to Jerusalem nor the Camp David Peace Agreement would have been possible. The fact that each side interpreted the agreement differently, depending on their point of view, was something he had both foreseen and taken into consideration, as had his American interlocutors, who pressed Begin and Sadat into accepting it.

Whether he would have been able to continue along the same lines and move towards a definite solution is more doubtful. Unlike Begin and Sharon, though, there is no question that he would have tried, and indeed being allowed to do so was his fondest wish. Certainly he was not prepared to give away anything that might endanger Israeli security which, as he saw it, dictated that the IDF remain on the watershed it had captured in 1967. On the other hand, he well realized that indefinite occupation was unsustainable and had to be terminated by whatever means were available: even if doing so would have meant direct talks with representatives of the Palestinian Liberation Organization, at the time an inconceivable proposition; even if it would have meant making far-reaching territorial concessions; and even if it would have meant some kind of arrangement concerning Jerusalem.

As he was mulling over these problems and trying to gather support for his views, the Israel he was slowly leaving behind was becoming a stranger and stranger place. Shortly after Dayan, Weizman too deserted Begin's cabinet. Like Dayan, he had started life as a hawk and gradually shifted to a more dove-like position. Like Dayan, he felt that the Prime Minister, far from trying to solve the Palestinian problem, was doing what he could to prevent it from being solved. Generals and brothers-in-law, they also had in common the fact that they both spoke Arabic and neither saw the Arabs as being either stupid or wicked. Begin, though, was not deterred: indeed, he was turning into a caricature of himself. More and more often he was carried away by his own rhetoric, such as when he called the PLO fighters in Lebanon 'biped animals'. Yet he was extremely popular; to the point that, when food earmarked for him was passed in procession through the streets of Jerusalem, people stood still and applauded.

At the same time, inflation was soaring into three figures. It became impossible to carry out the smallest transaction without first checking on the value of the dollar, which was serving as a ghost currency the value of which was rising day by day. This made the banks into some sort of secular temples; every morning crowds of people gathered around them, waiting for the doors to open so that speculation could start. Another factor in the equation was the IDF. Since 1973 it had been built up into a true juggernaut. It gobbled up the country's resources (as living standards and life expectancy increased the policy of early retirement, originally instituted by Dayan, became more and more expensive), and formed an almost intolerable burden. Now it was positively roaring to demonstrate its power. When Sharon was appointed Minister of Defence in Begin's second cabinet in the summer of 1981, he claimed it was capable of overrunning the entire region 'from the Atlantic to the Persian Gulf'.[106] Each time an incident took place somewhere, the entire General Staff would swoop down to see whether it might not be used as an excuse to blame Lebanon and invade it.

Dayan saw what was coming and tried to prevent it. In the spring of 1978, in response to a particularly vicious terrorist act, Israel had mounted a much smaller attack on Lebanon; in his memoirs he wrote that the operation, though 'necessary for defence', would not be registered 'among the more brilliant and sophisticated of the IDF's battles'. Many years previously Dayan had sought to teach the IDF about heroism. Now, in an attempt to minimize friendly casualties while fighting an enemy incomparably weaker than itself, the same IDF had advanced slowly and methodically behind a heavy artillery barrage. As a result, 'the only terrorists it caught and killed where those who chose to stay behind and fight'.[107] The rest fled, only to return as soon as the IDF pulled back and resume the same activities that had led to the strike initially. As usual, those who paid the price were the local inhabitants. Tens of thousands were forced to flee, and many suffered heavy damage to their property. It was as if the war in Vietnam, which he had observed at such close quarters and which he had considered unwinnable, had come to Israel; the main difference was that things were taking place not in some remote and unknown country but right next door. In the early summer of 1981 Dayan warned Begin against Sharon's Lebanese plans. Perhaps he remembered how, as a young hothead a quarter of a century earlier, he himself had nudged Ben Gurion into the Sinai Campaign; and how disappointed he had been when Israel proved to be unable to retain any of the gains it had made.

Aware that he was dying, what worried him most was the future of his country. Sadat's assassination, which took place only ten days before his own death, came as a shock. In the event, thanks largely to the fact that the Egyptian people were tired of war, the Camp David Agreements held. However, the warmth that marked its first years has long since gone; should a solution not be found to the Palestinian problem, the possibility of a major regional war breaking out between the two states cannot be ruled out. More important still, events have made it abundantly clear that Dayan's premonition that the occupation of the territories was untenable in the long run was correct. Had he witnessed today's uprising – in which Israeli tanks charge children with nothing but rocks in their hands and in which Palestinian casualties exceed Jewish ones by between four and five to one – he might even have found a new poignancy in the verses of his favourite poet, Nathan Alterman. In the last book he wrote, Dayan quotes Alterman as follows:[108]

> In blood the mothers stand,
> But no people are vanquished long
> If vanquished on their own land
> They rise ten times as strong.

The other thing that made him worry was the future of Rahel. During the difficult years after 1973 they had grown much closer than before, and in the various books he wrote he repeatedly refers to her ability to understand him without words. In some of his letters he called her '*ketzele*', which is Yiddish for kitten; a rather strange name to give an aristocratic, cool, and self-possessed woman. Be this as it may, given a pot of soup on the fire and a croissant to eat, in her company he was content. Since she did not have rich parents to fall back on, she made him feel needed in a way Ruth never had.

Whether for this reason or because it was his last opportunity to wield power, he played with several drafts of his will, devising ways of distributing his real estate, pensions, book-royalties, and antiques. Finally, though both of his sons were insolvent, he left Rahel practically everything he owned. His estate was valued at $2–2.5 million – a lot of money in the Israel of that time, although politicians less famous than he have been known to amass more. However numerous the antiques he took, he was never accused of financial wrongdoing. Of Dayan's estate no more than $150,000 went to his children, and even that they only got after they threatened to contest the will. In her book about him Yael took him to task for the way he divided his assets, but in the end she more or less accepted the *fait accompli*. Not so Ehud and Asaf. In October 2001, at a conference held to mark the twentieth anniversary of his death, they did not present themselves. However, a year later Asaf published an interview in which he bitterly regretted having given his father 'hell'; too late, as he himself said.

On 16 October 1981, to use the Biblical phrase he liked to quote, Dayan was 'gathered to his fathers'. As so often during his life, several women claimed possession over him. Yael, in her memoirs, wrote that both she and Rahel were present and that each of them occupied one side of his bed. Rahel, in one of her rare interviews, did not mention her step-daughter at all. Even Ms Mor suddenly reappeared out of nowhere; she offered Rahel to write a 'great book' about her but was sent packing. The object of their affections and their jealousy was buried at Nahalal near his parents, his brother who had been killed, his sister who had committed suicide, and ordinary *moshav* people with whom he had grown up and with whom, claiming to be a simple farmer at heart, he identified. The mourners included, in a great and almost unique honour, an official Egyptian delegation. He had asked there should be no official ceremony – to which, as a former chief of staff and cabinet minister, he was entitled – and no eulogies. It was a last gesture of contempt, but his wishes were respected. Right to the end, he had done it his way.

Endnotes

1 I wish to thank Mr Zeev Elron for his useful criticism of the first draft of this book.

2 S. Dayan, *Degania, Twenty-Five Years* [Hebrew], Tel Aviv, Stiebel, 1925, p. 85.

3 D. Dayan, *In Happiness and Sorrow* [Hebrew], Tel Aviv, Masada, 1958, p. 376.

4 J. Gefen, *Precious Woman* [Hebrew], Tel Aviv, Schocken, 1999, p. 103.

5 J. Shapira, *Nahalal* [Hebrew], Tel Aviv, Am Oved, 1946, p. 98.

6 D. Dayan, *In Happiness and Sorrow*, p. 110.

7 N. Ben Ari, ed., *My Ruth: Letters of Dayan from Acre Jail* [Hebrew], Tel Aviv, Zmora Bitan, 2001, p. 11.

8 Shapira, *Nahalal*, p. 127.

9 R. Dayan, *And Perhaps? The Story of Ruth Dayan* [Hebrew], Tel Aviv, Maariv, 1973, p. 59.

10 R. Dayan, *And Perhaps?*, p. 69.

11 Ben Ari, ed., *My Ruth* p. 117, letter of 8.3.1940.

12 Rabbi Tsvi H. Kalisher quoted in G, Kresel, *Rabi Yehuda Alkalai–Rabbi Tsvi Hirsh Kalischer* [Hebrew], Tel Aviv, Shreberk, n.d., p. 138.

13 A. Sharon, *Warrior: The Autobiography of Ariel Sharon*, New York, N.Y., Simon & Schuster, 1989, p. 73.

14 M. Dayan, *Autobiography* [Hebrew], Tel Aviv, Dvir, 1976, p. 36.

15 Printed in Ben Ari, ed., *My Ruth*, p. 26.

16 Ben Ari, ed., *My Ruth*, p. 44, letter of 16.12.1939.

17 M. Carmel, *Inside the Walls* [Hebrew], En Harod, Hakibbutz Hameuhad, p. 34.

18 Field Marshal John Dill, Chief of the Imperial General Staff, 1941, quoted in
    L. James, *Imperial Rearguard: Wars of Empire, 1919–1985*, London, Brassey's,
    1988, p. 96.
19 Ben Ari, ed., *My Ruth*, p. 95, letter of 15.2.1940.
20 *Ibid*, p. 174, letter of 10.6.1940.
21 *Ibid*, p. 237.
22 M. Dayan, *Autobiography*, p. 48.
23 Private communication from the late Dr J. Muggia, psychiatrist.
24 Letter to N. Betzer, 14.12.1945, quoted in S. Teveth, *Moshe Dayan, A
    Biography* [Hebrew], Tel Aviv, Schocken, 1973, p. 241.
25 See the episode as reported in Teveth, *Moshe Dayan*, p. 469.
26 Printed in E. Ben Ezer, *Courage: The Story of Moshe Dayan* [Hebrew], Tel
    Aviv, Ministry of Defence, 1997, p. 318. The translation is mine.
27 Teveth, *Moshe Dayan*, p. 264; that this was not just a phrase uttered during a
    moment of overconfidence is made clear by Y. Dayan, *My Father, His
    Daughter*, Jerusalem, Steimatzky, 1985, p. 62.
28 Teveth, *Moshe Dayan*, pp. 279–80.
29 Quoted in Z. Dror, *Commander without Authority: The Story of Yitzhak
    Sadeh* [Hebrew], Tel Aviv, Hakibbutz Hameuhad, 1996, p. 395.
30 M. Dayan, *Autobiography*, p. 62.
31 Y. Rabin, *Notebook* [Hebrew], Tel Aviv, Maariv, 1979, vol. 1, p. 60.
32 Quoted in Teveth, *Moshe Dayan*, p. 296.
33 M. Dayan, *Autobiography*, p. 74.
34 Rabin, *Notebook*, vol. 1, p. 84.
35 Quoted in A. Busheri, 'The Security Concept of Yigal Allon as Compared to
    that of Ben Gurion's' [Hebrew], Ph.D Thesis submitted to the Hebrew
    University, Jerusalem, 2003, p. 112.
36 M. Dayan, *Autobiography*, p. 94.
37 Meeting of 18.6.1950, quoted in B. Morris, *Israel's Border Wars 1949–1956*,
    [Hebrew], Tel Aviv, Am Oved, 1996, p. 190.
38 IDF Archive, file 40/103/53, pp. 5–7.
39 M. Amit, *Head On*, [Hebrew], Or Yehuda, Hed Arzi, 1999, p. 86.
40 *Ibid*, quoted in *ibid*, p. 203; See also M. Sharet, *Personal Diary, 1953–57*
    [Hebrew], Tel Aviv, Maariv, 1978, entry for 26.10.1954, vol. 2, p. 595.

41 Quoted in E. Kafkafi, *Pinhas Lavon – Anti Messiah, a Biography* [Hebrew], Tel 'Aviv, Am Oved, 1998, p. 231.
42 *Sharet*, Personal Diary, entry for 10.1.1955, vol. 3, p. 639.
43 Sharon, *Warrior*, p. 75.
44 D. Horowitz, *Sky-Blue and Dust; a Portrait of the Generation of 1948* [Hebrew], Jerusalem, Keter, 1993, p. 122.
45 Diary of the Office of the Chief of Staff, 23.10.1955, printed in M. Bar On, *The Gates of Gaza: Israel's Defence and Foreign Policy, 1955–57* [Hebrew], Tel Aviv, Am Oved, 1992, p. 64.
46 M. Dayan, *Autobiography*, p. 262.
47 *Ibid*, p. 250.
48 M. Naor, *Laskov* [Hebrew], Tel Aviv, Ministry of Defence, 1988, p. 261.
49 S. Peres, *The Next Stage* [Hebrew], Tel Aviv, Am Hasefer, 1965, p. 125.
50 M. Heikal, *Cutting the Lion's Tail; Suez Through Egyptian Eyes*, New York, N.Y., Arbor House, 1987, pp. 177–78.
51 M. Dayan, *Sinai Diary*, London, Weidenfeld and Nicolson, 1965, p. 66.
52 General Staff Meeting, 14.10.1956, IDF Archive 776/58, p. 27.
53 Printed in M. Dayan, *Autobiography*, p. 375.
54 Quoted in Naor, *Laskov*, p.275.
55 Y. Dayan, *My Father, His Daughter*, p. 109.
56 M. Dayan, *Autobiography*, p. 377.
57 *Ibid*, p. 388.
58 Peres, *Battling for Peace*, p. 101.
59 Hadassa Mor, *Red-Hot Paths* [Hebrew], Tel Aviv, Kotz, 1963, p. 207.
60 M. Dayan, *Story of My Life*, London, Weidenfeld and Nicolson, 1976, p. 290.
61 Mor, *Red-Hot Paths*, p. 78.
62 Peres, *Battling for Peace*, p. 154.
63 Gefen, *Precious Woman*, pp. 65, 66.
64 M. Dayan, *Vietnam Diary* [Hebrew], Tel Aviv, Dvir, 1977, p. 9.
65 *Ibid*, p. 59.
66 Gen. (ret.) C. Krulak, telephone interview, 5.11.2001.
67 For these quotes see M. Dayan, *Story of My Life*, pp. 293–96.
68 M. Dayan, *Vietnam Diary*, p. 111.
69 'Annual Report on the Syrian Armed Forces', 21 January 1966, FO/371/186923.

70 The various statements have been taken from M.Gilboa, *Six Years and Six Days: the Origins and Course of the Six Day War* [Hebrew], Tel Aviv, Am Oved, 1969, pp. 98 and 101.

71 Peres, *Battling for Peace*, p. 166.

72 Quoted in Teveth, *Moshe Dayan*, p. 403.

73 Peres, *Battling for Peace*, p. 101.

74 See *Yediot Aharonot* [Hebrew], 27.4.1997, p. 3.

75 M. Dayan, *Autobiography*, p. 398.

76 Rabin, *Notebook*, vol. 1 p. 151.

77 Sharon, *Warrior*, p. 186.

78 R. Parker, 'The View from the State Department', in A. Susser, ed., *Six Days – Thirty Years: New Perspectives on the Six Day War*, Tel Aviv, Am Oved, 1999, p. 130.

79 Quoted in M. Meizel, *The Campaign for the Golan, June 1967* [Hebrew], Tel Aviv, Ministry of Defence, 2001, p. 266.

80 See M. B. Oren, *Six Days of War: June 1967 and the Making of the Modern Middle East*, New York, N.Y., Oxford University Press, 2002, p. 259.

81 Meizel, *The Campaign for the Golan*, p. 270.

82 *Maariv*, 9.6.1967, p. 1.

83 Y. Dayan, *My Father, His Daughter*, p. 203.

84 20.6.1967.

85 General Haim Herzog as quoted in R. Slater, *Soldier, Warrior, Statesman: The Life of Moshe Dayan*, New York, N.Y., St. Martin's 1991, p. 292–93.

86 J. Alsop, 'Moshe Dayan's Motto', *Washington Post*, 8.12.1967.

87 Rabin, *Notebook*, vol. 1, p. 276.

88 M. Heikal, *The Road to Ramadan*, London, Fontana, 1975, p. 85.

89 Prof. Y. Ginat, Moshe Dayan Memorial Conference, Haifa University, 17.10.2001.

90 Y. Dayan, *My Father, His Daughter*, p. 230.

91 Quoted in A. Braun, *Moshe Dayan in the Yom Kippur War* [Hebrew], Tel Aviv, Idanim, 1992, p. 21.

92 Meeting of 18.4.1973, quoted in Braun, *Moshe Dayan*, p. 22.

93 Quoted in Braun, *Moshe Dayan*, p. 28.

94 Quoted in Braun, *Moshe Dayan*, p. 52.

95 E. Zeira, *The October 73 War: Myth Against Reality*, Tel Aviv, Yediot Aharonot, 1993, p. 181.

96 E. Haber, *Today War Will Break Out*, [Hebew] Tel Aviv, Idanim, 1987, pp. 16, 28.

97 M. Dayan, *Autobiography*, p. 662.

98 Quoted in Braun, *Moshe Dayan*, p. 176.

99 G. Meir, My Life, *London, Futura*, 1975, p. 239.

100 M. Dayan, *Shall the Sword Devour Forever?* [Hebrew], Tel Aviv, Idanim, 1981, p. 37.

101 W. Quandt, *Camp David: Peacemaking and Politics*, Washington DC, Brookings, 1986, p. 134.

102 Letter from Begin and Sadat to Carter, printed in W. B. Quandt, *Camp David: Peacemaking and Politics*, Washington DC, Brookings, 1986, pp. 402–3.

103 Speech of 6.3.1981, in M. Dayan, *On the Peace Process and the Future of Israel* [Hebrew], N. Yanai, ed., Tel Aviv, Ministry of Defence, p. 254.

104 Speech of 24.10.1980, *ibid*, p. 246.

105 M. Dayan, *Shall the Sword Devour Forever?*, pp. 243–44.

106 *Ma'ariv*, 18.2.1982, p. 1.

107 M. Dayan, *Shall the Sword Devour Forever?*, p. 107.

108 M. Dayan, *Living with the Bible*, London, Bantam, 1979, p. 156.

Bibliography

ENGLISH LANGUAGE ONLY

Almog, O., *Sabra: The Creation of the New Jew*, Berkeley, University of California Press, 2000. A sociological study of how the new Jew, of whom Dayan was the prototype, was created.

Bar On, M., *The Gates of Gaza: Israel's Road to Suez and Back, 1955-57*, New York, N.Y., St. Martin's, 1994. By the then manager of Dayan's office.

Ben Eliezer, U., *The Making of Israeli Militarism*, Bloomington, ID., Indiana University Press, 1998. Very good on the spirit in which Israel fought the Arabs.

Blum, H., *Eve of Destruction: The Untold Story of the Yom Kippur War*, New York, N.Y., HarperCollins, 2003. The most up to date account.

Dayan, M., *Living with the Bible*, London, Bantam, 1979. His most finely-crafted work; makes love to the country and its people.

Dayan, M., *Story of My Life*, London, Weidenfed & Nicolson, 1976. Leaves out many of the documents that dot the Hebrew version. Very well written but not always reliable.

Dayan, M., *Sinai Diary*, London, Weidenfeld & Nicolson, 1965. Well written but one sided.

Dayan, Y., *My Father, His Daughter*, Jerusalem, Steimatzky, 1985. A personal memoir by Dayan's favorite daughter.

Golan, M., *Israel in Search of a War: The Sinai Campaign, 1955–1956*, Brighton, Sussex Academic Press, 1998. How Dayan and Ben Gurion did not rest until they got the war they wanted.

Morris, B., *Israel's Border Wars, 1949–1956*, Oxford, Clarendon, 1993. Controversial work on a controversial period in which Dayan played a key part.

Oren, M. B., *Six Days of War: June 1967 and the Making of the Modern Middle East*, Oxford, Oxford University Press, 2002. Up to date and very detailed, if a bit journalistic.

Peres, S., *Battling for Peace*, London, Weidenfeld & Nicolson, 1995. The autobiography of one of the key figures in Israeli politics who knew Dayan well.

Rabin, Y., *The Rabin Memoirs*, Boston, MA., Little, Brown, 1979. Not terribly interesting, but informative on the 1967 War in particular.

Sharon, A., *Warrior: The Autobiography of Ariel Sharon*, New York, N.Y., Simon & Schuster, 1989. A personal account by one who worked under Dayan for many years.

Shlaim, A., *The Iron Wall: Israel and the Arab World*, New York, N.Y., Norton, 2000. As good a history of the Arab-Israeli conflict as there is, albeit with an anti-Israeli slant.

Slater, R., *Soldier, Warrior, Statesman: The Life of Moshe Dayan*, New York, N.Y., St. Martin's 1991. Solid, reliable piece of work.

Thomas, B., *How Israel Was Won: A Concise History of the Arab-Israeli Conflict*, Lanham, MD, Lexington, 1999. Balances Shlaim's work.

Van Creveld, M., *The Sword and the Olive: A Critical History of the Israel Defense Force*, New York, N.Y., Public Affairs, 2nd edition, 2002. The most comprehensive single account to date.

Index